Individual Studies for Grade 3

*A Year of Lesson Plans
for Language Arts, Math, and Science*

by
Sonya Shafer

Individual Studies for Grade 3: A Year of Lesson Plans for Language Arts, Math, and Science
© 2015, Sonya Shafer

All rights reserved. However, we grant permission to make printed copies or use this work on multiple electronic devices for members of your immediate household. Quantity discounts are available for classroom and co-op use. Please contact us for details.

Cover Design: John Shafer and Sarah Shafer

ISBN 978-1-61634-310-1 printed
ISBN 978-1-61634-311-8 electronic download

Published by
Simply Charlotte Mason, LLC
930 New Hope Road #11-892
Lawrenceville, Georgia 30045
simplycharlottemason.com

Printed by PrintLogic, Inc.
Monroe, Georgia, USA

Contents

How to Use 7
Complete Year's Resources List 8

Term 1 9

    Lesson 1 11
    Lesson 2 11
    Lesson 3 12
    Lesson 4 12
    Lesson 5 13
    Lesson 6 14
    Lesson 7 14
    Lesson 8 14
    Lesson 9 15
    Lesson 10 15
    Lesson 11 16
    Lesson 12 16
    Lesson 13 17
    Lesson 14 17
    Lesson 15 18
    Lesson 16 18
    Lesson 17 19
    Lesson 18 19
    Lesson 19 19
    Lesson 20 20
    Lesson 21 20
    Lesson 22 20
    Lesson 23 21
    Lesson 24 21
    Lesson 25 22
    Lesson 26 22
    Lesson 27 22
    Lesson 28 23
    Lesson 29 23
    Lesson 30 24
    Lesson 31 24
    Lesson 32 24
    Lesson 33 25
    Lesson 34 25
    Lesson 35 25
    Lesson 36 26
    Lesson 37 26
    Lesson 38 27
    Lesson 39 27
    Lesson 40 27
    Lesson 41 28
    Lesson 42 28

Lesson 43 29
Lesson 44 29
Lesson 45 29
Lesson 46 30
Lesson 47 30
Lesson 48 31
Lesson 49 31
Lesson 50 31
Lesson 51 32
Lesson 52 32
Lesson 53 33
Lesson 54 33
Lesson 55 33
Lesson 56 34
Lesson 57 34
Lesson 58 35
Lesson 59 35
Lesson 60 35

Term 2 .... *37*
Lesson 61 39
Lesson 62 39
Lesson 63 39
Lesson 64 40
Lesson 65 40
Lesson 66 41
Lesson 67 41
Lesson 68 41
Lesson 69 42
Lesson 70 42
Lesson 71 43
Lesson 72 43
Lesson 73 43
Lesson 74 44
Lesson 75 44
Lesson 76 45
Lesson 77 45
Lesson 78 45
Lesson 79 46
Lesson 80 46
Lesson 81 47
Lesson 82 47
Lesson 83 48
Lesson 84 48
Lesson 85 48
Lesson 86 49
Lesson 87 49
Lesson 88 50
Lesson 89 50

Lesson 90 50
Lesson 91 51
Lesson 92 51
Lesson 93 52
Lesson 94 52
Lesson 95 52
Lesson 96 53
Lesson 97 53
Lesson 98 54
Lesson 99 54
Lesson 100 54
Lesson 101 55
Lesson 102 55
Lesson 103 56
Lesson 104 56
Lesson 105 56
Lesson 106 57
Lesson 107 57
Lesson 108 58
Lesson 109 58
Lesson 110 59
Lesson 111 59
Lesson 112 59
Lesson 113 60
Lesson 114 60
Lesson 115 61
Lesson 116 61
Lesson 117 62
Lesson 118 62
Lesson 119 62
Lesson 120 63

Term 3 .... **65**
Lesson 121 67
Lesson 122 67
Lesson 123 67
Lesson 124 68
Lesson 125 68
Lesson 126 68
Lesson 127 69
Lesson 128 69
Lesson 129 70
Lesson 130 70
Lesson 131 70
Lesson 132 71
Lesson 133 71
Lesson 134 72
Lesson 135 72
Lesson 136 72

Lesson 137 73
Lesson 138 73
Lesson 139 74
Lesson 140 74
Lesson 141 74
Lesson 142 75
Lesson 143 75
Lesson 144 76
Lesson 145 76
Lesson 146 76
Lesson 147 77
Lesson 148 77
Lesson 149 78
Lesson 150 78
Lesson 151 78
Lesson 152 79
Lesson 153 79
Lesson 154 80
Lesson 155 80
Lesson 156 80
Lesson 157 81
Lesson 158 81
Lesson 159 82
Lesson 160 82
Lesson 161 82
Lesson 162 83
Lesson 163 83
Lesson 164 84
Lesson 165 84
Lesson 166 84
Lesson 167 85
Lesson 168 85
Lesson 169 86
Lesson 170 86
Lesson 171 86
Lesson 172 87
Lesson 173 87
Lesson 174 87
Lesson 175 88
Lesson 176 88
Lesson 177 88
Lesson 178 89
Lesson 179 89
Lesson 180 90

How to Use

Most school subjects can be taught to your whole family together, but some subjects are best taught individually so you can progress at the student's pace. This book of lesson plans contains suggestions and assignments for individual work for students in grade 3. Complete one lesson plan per day to finish these studies in a school year.

The lesson plans in this book cover language arts, science, and math.

Reading & Writing

Since students at this young age vary greatly in readiness for reading and writing, we offer two tracks of plans: A and B. Select the track that best fits your student and follow that track's plans throughout the year.

Track A—For students who would benefit from more reading practice and who are ready to learn cursive.

Track B—For students who would benefit from more reading practice or guided reading instruction (add the teacher book lessons) and more practice in either printing or cursive.

English

Students will progress in spelling, capitalization, punctuation, and English usage guidelines through the literary passages presented in *Spelling Wisdom, Book 1*, and the guided discovery lessons in *Using Language Well, Book 1*. The first half of these books will be covered this year, the rest in grade 4.

Science

Science can be done individually, or if you have more than one student in grades 1–6, they may all do one science course together. Simply Charlotte Mason has several to choose from.

Nature Study is an important part of science studies; be sure to include it. Follow the Nature Study suggestions in your selected science course or use the nature notebook, *Journaling a Year in Nature*, to guide your weekly study. Nature Study can be done all together as a family, but we have included reminders in these individual plans too.

Math

Use the math curriculum of your choice. These lesson plans will include reminders to work on it. As with other individual work, be sure to go at your student's pace.

simplycharlottemason.com

Complete Year's Resources List

- Math course of choice
- Simply Charlotte Mason science course of choice
- *Journaling a Year in Nature* notebooks, one per person (optional)
- *Spelling Wisdom, Book 1*
  Students will complete the first half of this book this year, the rest in grade 4.
- *Using Language Well, Book 1, Student Book*
  Students will complete the first half of the student book this year, the rest in grade 4.
- *Using Language Well, Book 1, Teacher Guide and Answer Key*

Select Track A *or* Track B

Track A
- *New Friends*
- *More New Friends*
- *Print to Cursive Proverbs*
  Print to Cursive Proverbs is available in two handwriting styles: the traditional print-straight-up-and-down Zaner Bloser and the print-on-a-slant D'Nealian. Select whichever style your student has learned to print in.

Track B
- *Hymns in Prose for Children*
- *Hymns in Prose Teacher Book* (optional)
  If your student simply needs reading practice, you will not need the teacher book. If your student needs more guided reading instruction, the teacher book will show you how to use *Hymns in Prose for Children* for structured reading lessons.
- *Hymns in Prose Copybook*
  The *Hymns in Prose Copybook* is available in printing or in cursive and in your choice of two styles: the traditional print-straight-up-and-down Zaner Bloser and the print-on-a-slant D'Nealian. Select whichever style your student has learned to write in.

Note: All resources except math are available from Simply Charlotte Mason.

Term 1
(12 weeks; 5 lessons/week)

Term 1 Resources List
- *Spelling Wisdom, Book 1*
- *Using Language Well, Book 1, Student Book*
- *Using Language Well, Book 1, Teacher Guide and Answer Key*
- Math course of choice
- Simply Charlotte Mason (SCM) science course of choice
- *Journaling a Year in Nature* notebooks (optional)

Track A
- *Print to Cursive Proverbs*
- *New Friends*

Track B
- *Hymns in Prose for Children*
- *Hymns in Prose Teacher Book* (optional)
- *Hymns in Prose Copybook*

Weekly Schedule

	Day One	Day Two	Day Three	Day Four	Day Five
	Math (20 min.)	Math (20 min.)	Math (20 min.)	Math (20 min.)	Math (20 min.)
		Science (15–20 min.)		Science (15–20 min.)	(Nature Study)
	Spelling Wisdom & Using Language Well (10–15 min.)				Spelling Wisdom & Using Language Well (10–15 min.)
Track A	New Friends (10–15 min.)	Print to Cursive Proverbs (5–10 min.)	New Friends (10–15 min.)	Print to Cursive Proverbs (5–10 min.)	Print to Cursive Proverbs (5–10 min.)
Track B		Hymns in Prose (5–15 min.)	Hymns in Prose (5–10 min.)	(opt.) Hymns in Prose (15 min.)	

TERM 1

Lesson 1

Materials Needed
- *Spelling Wisdom, Book 1*
- *Using Language Well, Book 1, Student Book*
- *Using Language Well, Book 1, Teacher Guide and Answer Key*
- Math course of choice
- *New Friends* (Track A)

English: Complete *Using Language Well, Book 1*, Lesson 1.

Tip: Most of the lessons assigned in Using Language Well, Book 1, *for grade 3 can be done orally in five minutes or less, leaving only the transcription portions to be written.*

Math: Work on your selected math curriculum for about 20 minutes.

Track A: Have your student read aloud *New Friends,* pages 6–14, "Something Special."

Tip: Select either Track A or Track B to complete with your student. You need do only one. See page 7 for detailed descriptions.

Lesson 2

Materials Needed
- *Print to Cursive Proverbs* (Track A)
- *Hymns in Prose for Children* (Track B)
- *Hymns in Prose Teacher Book* (Track B, optional)
- Math course of choice
- SCM science course of choice

Track A: Have your student read aloud the proverb in *Print to Cursive Proverbs,* pages 5 and 6, then carefully copy it. Encourage him to pay close attention as he copies, for when he is done you will ask him how to spell one of the words. When he has finished the copywork, invite him first to spell any word he remembers from the passage. Ask him to spell *work*; if he is unsure, allow him to look at the word.

Tip: Feel free to jot down his selected words over in the Notes column so you can easily refer to them for periodic reviews.

Track B: If your student needs more guided reading instruction, spend 15 minutes working on a lesson from the *Hymns in Prose Teacher Book.*

Notes

simplycharlottemason.com

11

TERM 1

Notes

If your student simply needs reading practice, have him read aloud Hymn 1 in *Hymns in Prose for Children.*

Tip: A good way to tell whether your student would benefit from more reading instruction or simply needs reading practice is to look over Hymn 1. If your student would be able to read most or all of it with no help from you, he probably just needs reading practice at this point. If, however, he would struggle to read Hymn 1 without help, you will want to follow the "guided reading instruction" cues in the Track B lesson plans in this book.

Math: Work on your selected math curriculum for about 20 minutes.

Science: In your SCM science course, complete the first assignment for Week 1.

Lesson 3

Materials Needed
- Math course of choice
- *New Friends* (Track A)
- *Hymns in Prose Copybook* (Track B)

Math: Work on your selected math curriculum for about 20 minutes.

Track A: Have your student read aloud *New Friends*, pages 15–21, "Something Special (Part 2)."

Track B: Have your student carefully copy *Hymns in Prose Copybook*, page 5. Encourage him to pay close attention as he copies, for when he is done you will ask him to select a phrase from the passage to write from memory. Allow him to look at the phrase until he is sure he can spell each word in it correctly. A phrase of about three or four words would be ideal, but allow him to select as much as he can accomplish correctly.

Tip: Make a note of his selected phrases in the sidebar of this book so you will have them handy for periodic reviews.

Lesson 4

Materials Needed
- *Print to Cursive Proverbs* (Track A)
- *Hymns in Prose Teacher Book* (Track B, optional)
- Math course of choice
- SCM science course of choice

Track A: Have your student read aloud the proverb at the top of *Print to Cursive*

12   *simplycharlottemason.com*

Proverbs, page 7, then complete the page.

Track B: If your student needs more guided reading instruction, spend 15 minutes working on a lesson from the *Hymns in Prose Teacher Book*.

Math: Work on your selected math curriculum for about 20 minutes.

Science: In your SCM science course, complete the second assignment for Week 1.

Tip: You may complete school assignments in any order that works best for your family's schedule. Try to sequence lessons throughout the day to use different parts of the student's brain and body as you go along. In other words, don't schedule two "book-heavy" assignments back to back. Put the math assignment in between or do some Family work—such as Picture Study or Music Study—in between to break up the readings. Each lesson plan in this book is sequenced to help you with that important principle.

Lesson 5

Materials Needed
- *Print to Cursive Proverbs* (Track A)
- Math course of choice
- *Spelling Wisdom, Book 1*
- *Using Language Well, Book 1, Student Book*
- *Using Language Well, Book 1, Teacher Guide and Answer Key*
- *Journaling a Year in Nature* notebooks (optional)

Track A: Have your student read aloud the proverb in *Print to Cursive Proverbs*, pages 8 and 9, then carefully copy it. Remind him to pay close attention as he copies, for when he is done you will ask him how to spell one of the words. When he has finished the copywork, invite him first to spell any word he remembers. Ask him to spell *good*; if he is unsure, allow him to look at the word.

Math: Work on your selected math curriculum for about 20 minutes.

English: Complete *Using Language Well, Book 1*, Lesson 2.

Nature Study: Take the whole family outside for nature study.

Tip: Follow the Nature Study suggestions in your SCM science course or use the nature notebooks, Journaling a Year in Nature, *to guide your weekly study.*

TERM 1

Notes

Lesson 6

Materials Needed
- *Spelling Wisdom, Book 1*
- *Using Language Well, Book 1, Student Book*
- *Using Language Well, Book 1, Teacher Guide and Answer Key*
- Math course of choice
- *New Friends* (Track A)

English: Complete *Using Language Well, Book 1,* Lesson 3.

Math: Work on your selected math curriculum for about 20 minutes.

Track A: Have your student read aloud *New Friends,* pages 22–30, "What Is a Habit?"

Lesson 7

Materials Needed
- *Print to Cursive Proverbs* (Track A)
- *Hymns in Prose Copybook* (Track B)
- *Hymns in Prose Teacher Book* (Track B, optional)
- Math course of choice
- SCM science course of choice

Track A: Have your student read aloud the proverb at the top of *Print to Cursive Proverbs,* page 10, then complete the page.

Track B: Have your student carefully copy *Hymns in Prose Copybook,* page 6. Ask him to select a phrase from the passage to write from memory. Allow him to look at the phrase until he is sure he can spell each word in it correctly.

If your student needs more guided reading instruction, spend 15 minutes working on a lesson from the *Hymns in Prose Teacher Book.*

Tip: You may want to separate the copywork from the reading lesson in order not to fatigue that part of your student's brain. Inserting a lesson of a completely different nature—such as math or picture study—between the two lessons will help him pay full attention for both.

Math: Work on your selected math curriculum for about 20 minutes.

Science: In your SCM science course, complete the first assignment for Week 2.

Lesson 8

Materials Needed
- Math course of choice

simplycharlottemason.com

- *New Friends* (Track A)
- *Hymns in Prose Copybook* (Track B)

Math: Work on your selected math curriculum for about 20 minutes.

Track A: Have your student read aloud *New Friends,* pages 30–40, "Dad Keeps His Promise."

Track B: Have your student carefully copy *Hymns in Prose Copybook,* page 7. Ask him to select a phrase from the passage to write from memory. Allow him to look at the phrase until he is sure he can spell each word in it correctly.

Lesson 9

Materials Needed
- *Print to Cursive Proverbs* (Track A)
- *Hymns in Prose Teacher Book* (Track B, optional)
- Math course of choice
- SCM science course of choice

Track A: Have your student read aloud the proverb in *Print to Cursive Proverbs,* pages 11 and 12, then carefully copy it. When he has finished the copywork, invite him to spell any word he remembers. Ask him to spell *come;* if he is unsure, allow him to look at the word.

Tip: Encourage the habits of attention and best effort in copywork lessons by expecting it to be done right the first time. Mistakes or sloppy work requires the student to recopy the entire passage until it is done well.

Track B: If your student needs more guided reading instruction, spend 15 minutes working on a lesson from the *Hymns in Prose Teacher Book.*

Math: Work on your selected math curriculum for about 20 minutes.

Science: In your SCM science course, complete the second assignment for Week 2.

Lesson 10

Materials Needed
- *Print to Cursive Proverbs* (Track A)
- Math course of choice
- *Spelling Wisdom, Book 1*
- *Using Language Well, Book 1, Student Book*
- *Using Language Well, Book 1, Teacher Guide and Answer Key*
- *Journaling a Year in Nature* notebooks (optional)

simplycharlottemason.com

TERM 1

Notes

Track A: Have your student read aloud the proverb at the top of *Print to Cursive Proverbs*, page 13, then complete the page.

Math: Work on your selected math curriculum for about 20 minutes.

English: Complete *Using Language Well, Book 1*, Lesson 4.

Nature Study: Take the whole family outside for nature study.

Tip: Follow the Nature Study suggestions in your SCM science course or use the nature notebooks, Journaling a Year in Nature, *to guide your weekly nature study.*

Lesson 11

Materials Needed
- *Spelling Wisdom, Book 1*
- *Using Language Well, Book 1, Student Book*
- *Using Language Well, Book 1, Teacher Guide and Answer Key*
- Math course of choice
- *New Friends* (Track A)

English: Complete *Using Language Well, Book 1*, Lesson 5.

Math: Work on your selected math curriculum for about 20 minutes.

Track A: Have your student read aloud *New Friends,* pages 41–52, "Help for Rachel's Habit."

Tip: The poems sprinkled throughout New Friends *are optional. You may have your student read them or skip them. They will not be scheduled into these plans. (We recommend you focus on one master poet for the entire year, reading aloud one of his poems each week for the whole family. Details are given in SCM's Enrichment lesson plan books and* Enjoy the Poems *series.)*

Lesson 12

Materials Needed
- *Print to Cursive Proverbs* (Track A)
- *Hymns in Prose Copybook* (Track B)
- *Hymns in Prose Teacher Book* (Track B, optional)
- Math course of choice
- SCM science course of choice

simplycharlottemason.com

Track A: Have your student read aloud the proverb in *Print to Cursive Proverbs*, pages 14 and 15, then carefully copy it. When he has finished the copywork, invite him to spell any word he remembers. Ask him to spell *fear*; if he is unsure, allow him to look at the word.

Track B: Have your student carefully copy *Hymns in Prose Copybook*, page 8. Ask him to select a phrase from the passage to write from memory. Allow him to look at the phrase until he is sure he can spell each word in it correctly.

If your student needs more guided reading instruction, spend 15 minutes working on a lesson from the *Hymns in Prose Teacher Book*.

Math: Work on your selected math curriculum for about 20 minutes.

Science: In your SCM science course, complete the first assignment for Week 3.

Tip: Oral narration lays the foundation for solid composition skills. Make sure your student is giving several oral narrations each week from his history, science, geography, or Bible readings. (Download the free e-book, Five Steps to Successful Narration, *at simplycm.com/fivesteps for helpful how-to's.)*

Lesson 13

Materials Needed
- Math course of choice
- *New Friends,* if needed (Track A)
- *Hymns in Prose Copybook* (Track B)

Math: Work on your selected math curriculum for about 20 minutes.

Track A: Use today to catch up on any assigned reading in *New Friends,* as needed.

Track B: Have your student carefully copy *Hymns in Prose Copybook*, page 9. Ask him to select a phrase from the passage to write from memory. Allow him to look at the phrase until he is sure he can spell each word in it correctly.

Lesson 14

Materials Needed
- *Print to Cursive Proverbs* (Track A)
- *Hymns in Prose Teacher Book* (Track B, optional)
- Math course of choice
- SCM science course of choice

Track A: Have your student read aloud the proverb at the top of *Print to Cursive Proverbs*, page 16, then complete the page.

TERM 1

Notes

Track B: If your student needs more guided reading instruction, spend 15 minutes working on a lesson from the *Hymns in Prose Teacher Book*.

Math: Work on your selected math curriculum for about 20 minutes.

Science: In your SCM science course, complete the second assignment for Week 3.

Lesson 15

Materials Needed
- *Print to Cursive Proverbs* (Track A)
- Math course of choice
- *Spelling Wisdom, Book 1*
- *Using Language Well, Book 1, Student Book*
- *Using Language Well, Book 1, Teacher Guide and Answer Key*
- *Journaling a Year in Nature* notebooks (optional)

Track A: Have your student read aloud the proverb in *Print to Cursive Proverbs,* page 17, then carefully copy it. When he has finished the copywork, invite him to spell any word he remembers. Ask him to spell *before*; if he is unsure, allow him to look at the word.

Math: Work on your selected math curriculum for about 20 minutes.

English: Complete *Using Language Well, Book 1,* Lesson 6.

Nature Study: Take the whole family outside for nature study.

Tip: Follow the Nature Study suggestions in your SCM science course or use the nature notebooks, Journaling a Year in Nature, *to guide your weekly nature study.*

Lesson 16

Materials Needed
- *Spelling Wisdom, Book 1*
- *Using Language Well, Book 1, Student Book*
- *Using Language Well, Book 1, Teacher Guide and Answer Key*
- Math course of choice
- *New Friends* (Track A)

English: Complete *Using Language Well, Book 1,* Lesson 7.

Math: Work on your selected math curriculum for about 20 minutes.

Track A: Have your student read aloud *New Friends,* pages 58–66, "Tricked By a Bird."

TERM 1

Lesson 17

Materials Needed
- *Print to Cursive Proverbs,* if needed (Track A)
- *Hymns in Prose Copybook* (Track B)
- *Hymns in Prose Teacher Book* (Track B, optional)
- Math course of choice
- SCM science course of choice

Track A: Use today to catch up on any assigned pages in *Print to Cursive Proverbs,* as needed. If desired, review these words and your student's selected words from previous copywork lessons: *work, good, come, fear, before.* If your student is unsure about a particular word's spelling, allow him to look at the word.

Track B: Have your student carefully copy *Hymns in Prose Copybook,* page 10. Ask him to select a phrase from the passage to write from memory. Allow him to look at the phrase until he is sure he can spell each word in it correctly.

   If your student needs more guided reading instruction, spend 15 minutes working on a lesson from the *Hymns in Prose Teacher Book.*

Math: Work on your selected math curriculum for about 20 minutes.

Science: In your SCM science course, complete the first assignment for Week 4.

Lesson 18

Materials Needed
- Math course of choice
- *New Friends* (Track A)
- *Hymns in Prose Copybook* (Track B)

Math: Work on your selected math curriculum for about 20 minutes.

Track A: Have your student read aloud *New Friends,* pages 66–77, "Chee, the Barn Swallow."

Track B: Have your student carefully copy *Hymns in Prose Copybook,* page 11. Ask him to select a phrase from the passage to write from memory. Allow him to look at the phrase until he is sure he can spell each word in it correctly.

Lesson 19

Materials Needed
- *Print to Cursive Proverbs* (Track A)
- *Hymns in Prose Teacher Book* (Track B, optional)
- Math course of choice
- SCM science course of choice

Notes

simplycharlottemason.com

19

TERM 1

Notes

Track A: Have your student read aloud the proverb at the top of *Print to Cursive Proverbs,* page 18, then complete the page.

Track B: If your student needs more guided reading instruction, spend 15 minutes working on a lesson from the *Hymns in Prose Teacher Book.*

Math: Work on your selected math curriculum for about 20 minutes.

Science: In your SCM science course, complete the second assignment for Week 4.

Lesson 20

Materials Needed
- *Print to Cursive Proverbs* (Track A)
- Math course of choice
- *Spelling Wisdom, Book 1*
- *Using Language Well, Book 1, Student Book*
- *Using Language Well, Book 1, Teacher Guide and Answer Key*
- *Journaling a Year in Nature* notebooks (optional)

Track A: Have your student complete *Print to Cursive Proverbs,* page 19.

Math: Work on your selected math curriculum for about 20 minutes.

English: Complete *Using Language Well, Book 1,* Lesson 8.

Nature Study: Take the whole family outside for nature study.

Lesson 21

Materials Needed
- *Spelling Wisdom, Book 1*
- *Using Language Well, Book 1, Student Book*
- *Using Language Well, Book 1, Teacher Guide and Answer Key*
- Math course of choice
- *New Friends* (Track A)

English: Complete *Using Language Well, Book 1,* Lesson 9.

Math: Work on your selected math curriculum for about 20 minutes.

Track A: Have your student read aloud *New Friends,* pages 78–83, "Peggy, the Penguin."

Lesson 22

Materials Needed
- *Print to Cursive Proverbs* (Track A)

TERM 1

Notes

- *Hymns in Prose Copybook* (Track B)
- *Hymns in Prose Teacher Book* (Track B, optional)
- Math course of choice
- SCM science course of choice

Track A: Have your student read aloud the proverb in *Print to Cursive Proverbs,* page 20, then carefully copy it. When he has finished the copywork, invite him to spell any word he remembers. Ask him to spell *turns;* if he is unsure, allow him to look at the word.

Track B: Have your student carefully copy *Hymns in Prose Copybook,* page 12. Ask him to select a phrase from the passage to write from memory. Allow him to look at the phrase until he is sure he can spell each word in it correctly.

If your student needs more guided reading instruction, spend 15 minutes working on a lesson from the *Hymns in Prose Teacher Book.*

Math: Work on your selected math curriculum for about 20 minutes.

Science: In your SCM science course, complete the first assignment for Week 5.

Lesson 23

Materials Needed
- Math course of choice
- *New Friends* (Track A)
- *Hymns in Prose Copybook,* if needed (Track B)

Math: Work on your selected math curriculum for about 20 minutes.

Track A: Have your student read aloud *New Friends,* pages 84–88, "Whistle, the Baltimore Oriole."

Track B: Use today to catch up on any assigned pages in *Hymns in Prose Copybook,* as needed. If desired, review two or three of your student's selected phrases; see if he can write each phrase correctly as you read it to him.

Lesson 24

Materials Needed
- *Print to Cursive Proverbs* (Track A)
- *Hymns in Prose Teacher Book* (Track B, optional)
- Math course of choice
- SCM science course of choice

Track A: Have your student read aloud the proverb at the top of *Print to Cursive Proverbs,* page 21, then complete the page.

Track B: If your student needs more guided reading instruction, spend 15 minutes working on a lesson from the *Hymns in Prose Teacher Book.*

simplycharlottemason.com

Notes

Math: Work on your selected math curriculum for about 20 minutes.

Science: In your SCM science course, complete the second assignment for Week 5.

Lesson 25

Materials Needed
- *Print to Cursive Proverbs* (Track A)
- Math course of choice
- *Spelling Wisdom, Book 1*
- *Using Language Well, Book 1, Student Book*
- *Using Language Well, Book 1, Teacher Guide and Answer Key*
- *Journaling a Year in Nature* notebooks (optional)

Track A: Have your student complete *Print to Cursive Proverbs,* page 22.

Math: Work on your selected math curriculum for about 20 minutes.

English: Complete *Using Language Well, Book 1,* Lesson 10.

Nature Study: Take the whole family outside for nature study.

Lesson 26

Materials Needed
- *Spelling Wisdom, Book 1*
- *Using Language Well, Book 1, Student Book*
- *Using Language Well, Book 1, Teacher Guide and Answer Key*
- Math course of choice
- *New Friends* (Track A)

English: Complete *Using Language Well, Book 1,* Lesson 11.

Math: Work on your selected math curriculum for about 20 minutes.

Track A: Have your student read aloud *New Friends,* pages 89–93, "A Family of Pelicans."

Lesson 27

Materials Needed
- *Print to Cursive Proverbs* (Track A)
- *Hymns in Prose for Children* (Track B)
- *Hymns in Prose Teacher Book* (Track B, optional)
- Math course of choice
- SCM science course of choice

Track A: Have your student read aloud the proverb in *Print to Cursive Proverbs,* page 23, then carefully copy it. When he has finished the copywork, invite him to spell any word he remembers. Ask him to spell *wise*; if he is unsure, allow him to look at the word.

Track B: If your student needs more guided reading instruction, spend 15 minutes working on a lesson from the *Hymns in Prose Teacher Book.*

If he simply needs practice reading, have your student read aloud *Hymns in Prose for Children,* Hymn 2.

Math: Work on your selected math curriculum for about 20 minutes.

Science: In your SCM science course, complete the first assignment for Week 6.

Lesson 28

Materials Needed
- Math course of choice
- *New Friends,* if needed (Track A)
- *Hymns in Prose for Children* (Track B)

Math: Work on your selected math curriculum for about 20 minutes.

Track A: Use today to catch up on any assigned reading in *New Friends,* as needed.

Track B: If your student simply needs more practice reading, have him read aloud *Hymns in Prose for Children,* Hymn 3. (If he needs more guided reading instruction, don't worry about reading this hymn right now. Your student will read the hymns as he progresses in his reading instruction lessons.)

Lesson 29

Materials Needed
- *Print to Cursive Proverbs* (Track A)
- *Hymns in Prose Teacher Book* (Track B, optional)
- Math course of choice
- SCM science course of choice

Track A: Have your student read aloud the proverb at the top of *Print to Cursive Proverbs,* page 24, then complete the page.

Track B: If your student needs more guided reading instruction, spend 15 minutes working on a lesson from the *Hymns in Prose Teacher Book.*

Math: Work on your selected math curriculum for about 20 minutes.

Science: In your SCM science course, complete the second assignment for Week 6.

Notes

Lesson 30

Materials Needed
- *Print to Cursive Proverbs* (Track A)
- Math course of choice
- *Spelling Wisdom, Book 1*
- *Using Language Well, Book 1, Student Book*
- *Using Language Well, Book 1, Teacher Guide and Answer Key*
- *Journaling a Year in Nature* notebooks (optional)

Track A: Have your student complete *Print to Cursive Proverbs,* page 25.

Math: Work on your selected math curriculum for about 20 minutes.

English: Complete *Using Language Well, Book 1,* Lesson 12.

Nature Study: Take the whole family outside for nature study.

Lesson 31

Materials Needed
- *Spelling Wisdom, Book 1*
- *Using Language Well, Book 1, Student Book*
- *Using Language Well, Book 1, Teacher Guide and Answer Key*
- Math course of choice
- *New Friends* (Track A)

English: Complete *Using Language Well, Book 1,* Lesson 13.

Math: Work on your selected math curriculum for about 20 minutes.

Track A: Have your student read aloud *New Friends,* pages 98–106, "Great Plans."

Lesson 32

Materials Needed
- *Print to Cursive Proverbs* (Track A)
- *Hymns in Prose for Children* (Track B)
- *Hymns in Prose Teacher Book* (Track B, optional)
- Math course of choice
- SCM science course of choice

Track A: Have your student read aloud the proverb in *Print to Cursive Proverbs,* pages 26 and 27, then carefully copy it. When he has finished the copywork, invite him to spell any word he remembers. Ask him to spell *false*; if he is unsure, allow him to look at the word.

Track B: If your student needs more guided reading instruction, spend 15 minutes working on a lesson from the *Hymns in Prose Teacher Book*.

If he simply needs practice reading, have your student read aloud *Hymns in Prose for Children*, Hymn 4.

Math: Work on your selected math curriculum for about 20 minutes.

Science: In your SCM science course, complete the first assignment for Week 7.

Lesson 33

Materials Needed
- Math course of choice
- *New Friends* (Track A)
- *Hymns in Prose Copybook* (Track B)

Math: Work on your selected math curriculum for about 20 minutes.

Track A: Have your student read aloud *New Friends*, pages 106–117, "The Surprise Cake."

Track B: Have your student carefully copy *Hymns in Prose Copybook*, page 13. Ask him to select a phrase from the passage to write from memory. Allow him to look at the phrase until he is sure he can spell each word in it correctly.

Lesson 34

Materials Needed
- *Print to Cursive Proverbs* (Track A)
- *Hymns in Prose Teacher Book* (Track B, optional)
- Math course of choice
- SCM science course of choice

Track A: Have your student read aloud the proverb at the top of *Print to Cursive Proverbs*, page 28, then complete the page.

Track B: If your student needs more guided reading instruction, spend 15 minutes working on a lesson from the *Hymns in Prose Teacher Book*.

Math: Work on your selected math curriculum for about 20 minutes.

Science: In your SCM science course, complete the second assignment for Week 7.

Lesson 35

Materials Needed
- *Print to Cursive Proverbs* (Track A)
- Math course of choice

TERM 1

Notes

- *Spelling Wisdom, Book 1*
- *Using Language Well, Book 1, Student Book*
- *Using Language Well, Book 1, Teacher Guide and Answer Key*
- *Journaling a Year in Nature* notebooks (optional)

Track A: Have your student complete *Print to Cursive Proverbs,* page 29.

Math: Work on your selected math curriculum for about 20 minutes.

English: Complete *Using Language Well, Book 1,* Lesson 14.

Nature Study: Take the whole family outside for nature study.

Lesson 36

Materials Needed
- *Spelling Wisdom, Book 1*
- *Using Language Well, Book 1, Student Book*
- *Using Language Well, Book 1, Teacher Guide and Answer Key*
- Math course of choice
- *New Friends* (Track A)

English: Complete *Using Language Well, Book 1,* Lesson 15.

Math: Work on your selected math curriculum for about 20 minutes.

Track A: Have your student read aloud *New Friends,* pages 118–127, "Greener Grass."

Lesson 37

Materials Needed
- *Print to Cursive Proverbs* (Track A)
- *Hymns in Prose Copybook* (Track B)
- *Hymns in Prose Teacher Book* (Track B, optional)
- Math course of choice
- SCM science course of choice

Track A: Have your student read aloud the proverb in *Print to Cursive Proverbs,* pages 30 and 31, then carefully copy it. When he has finished the copywork, invite him to spell any word he remembers. Ask him to spell *every*; if he is unsure, allow him to look at the word.

Track B: Have your student carefully copy *Hymns in Prose Copybook,* page 14. Ask him to select a phrase from the passage to write from memory. Allow him to look at the phrase until he is sure he can spell each word in it correctly.

If your student needs more guided reading instruction, spend 15 minutes working on a lesson from the *Hymns in Prose Teacher Book.*

26

simplycharlottemason.com

TERM 1

Notes

Math: Work on your selected math curriculum for about 20 minutes.

Science: In your SCM science course, complete the first assignment for Week 8.

Lesson 38

Materials Needed
- Math course of choice
- *New Friends* (Track A)
- *Hymns in Prose Copybook* (Track B)

Math: Work on your selected math curriculum for about 20 minutes.

Track A: Have your student read aloud *New Friends*, pages 127–137, "Work Before Play."

Track B: Have your student carefully copy *Hymns in Prose Copybook*, page 15. Ask him to select a phrase from the passage to write from memory. Allow him to look at the phrase until he is sure he can spell each word in it correctly.

Lesson 39

Materials Needed
- *Print to Cursive Proverbs* (Track A)
- *Hymns in Prose Teacher Book* (Track B, optional)
- Math course of choice
- SCM science course of choice

Track A: Have your student read aloud the proverb at the top of *Print to Cursive Proverbs*, page 32, then complete the page.

Track B: If your student needs more guided reading instruction, spend 15 minutes working on a lesson from the *Hymns in Prose Teacher Book*.

Math: Work on your selected math curriculum for about 20 minutes.

Science: In your SCM science course, complete the second assignment for Week 8.

Lesson 40

Materials Needed
- *Print to Cursive Proverbs* (Track A)
- Math course of choice
- *Spelling Wisdom, Book 1*
- *Using Language Well, Book 1, Student Book*
- *Using Language Well, Book 1, Teacher Guide and Answer Key*
- *Journaling a Year in Nature* notebooks (optional)

simplycharlottemason.com

27

TERM 1

Notes

Track A: Have your student complete *Print to Cursive Proverbs*, page 33.

Math: Work on your selected math curriculum for about 20 minutes.

English: Complete *Using Language Well, Book 1*, Lesson 16.

Nature Study: Take the whole family outside for nature study.

Lesson 41

Materials Needed
- *Spelling Wisdom, Book 1*
- *Using Language Well, Book 1, Student Book*
- *Using Language Well, Book 1, Teacher Guide and Answer Key*
- Math course of choice
- *New Friends* (Track A)

English: Complete *Using Language Well, Book 1*, Lesson 17.

Math: Work on your selected math curriculum for about 20 minutes.

Track A: Have your student read aloud *New Friends*, pages 138–148, "Ten Thousand Babies."

Lesson 42

Materials Needed
- *Print to Cursive Proverbs* (Track A)
- *Hymns in Prose Copybook* (Track B)
- *Hymns in Prose Teacher Book* (Track B, optional)
- Math course of choice
- SCM science course of choice

Track A: Have your student read aloud the proverb in *Print to Cursive Proverbs*, pages 34 and 35, then carefully copy it. When he has finished the copywork, invite him to spell any word he remembers. Ask him to spell *great*; if he is unsure, allow him to look at the word.

Track B: Have your student carefully copy *Hymns in Prose Copybook*, page 16. Ask him to select a phrase from the passage to write from memory. Allow him to look at the phrase until he is sure he can spell each word in it correctly.

If your student needs more guided reading instruction, spend 15 minutes working on a lesson from the *Hymns in Prose Teacher Book*.

Math: Work on your selected math curriculum for about 20 minutes.

Science: In your SCM science course, complete the first assignment for Week 9.

simplycharlottemason.com

TERM

Notes

Lesson 43

Materials Needed
- Math course of choice
- *New Friends,* if needed (Track A)
- *Hymns in Prose Copybook* (Track B)

Math: Work on your selected math curriculum for about 20 minutes.

Track A: Use today to catch up on any assigned reading in *New Friends,* as needed.

Track B: Have your student carefully copy *Hymns in Prose Copybook,* page 17. Ask him to select a phrase from the passage to write from memory. Allow him to look at the phrase until he is sure he can spell each word in it correctly.

Lesson 44

Materials Needed
- *Print to Cursive Proverbs* (Track A)
- *Hymns in Prose Teacher Book* (Track B, optional)
- Math course of choice
- SCM science course of choice

Track A: Have your student read aloud the proverb at the top of *Print to Cursive Proverbs,* page 36, then complete the page.

Track B: If your student needs more guided reading instruction, spend 15 minutes working on a lesson from the *Hymns in Prose Teacher Book.*

Math: Work on your selected math curriculum for about 20 minutes.

Science: In your SCM science course, complete the second assignment for Week 9.

Lesson 45

Materials Needed
- *Print to Cursive Proverbs* (Track A)
- Math course of choice
- *Spelling Wisdom, Book 1*
- *Using Language Well, Book 1, Student Book*
- *Using Language Well, Book 1, Teacher Guide and Answer Key*
- *Journaling a Year in Nature* notebooks (optional)

Track A: Have your student complete *Print to Cursive Proverbs,* page 37.

Math: Work on your selected math curriculum for about 20 minutes.

simplycharlottemason.com

Notes

English: Complete *Using Language Well, Book 1,* Lesson 18.

Nature Study: Take the whole family outside for nature study.

Lesson 46

Materials Needed
- *Spelling Wisdom, Book 1*
- *Using Language Well, Book 1, Student Book*
- *Using Language Well, Book 1, Teacher Guide and Answer Key*
- Math course of choice
- *New Friends* (Track A)

English: Complete *Using Language Well, Book 1,* Lesson 19.

Math: Work on your selected math curriculum for about 20 minutes.

Track A: Have your student read aloud *New Friends,* pages 152–158, "A Dollar to Spend."

Lesson 47

Materials Needed
- *Print to Cursive Proverbs* (Track A)
- *Hymns in Prose Copybook* (Track B)
- *Hymns in Prose Teacher Book* (Track B, optional)
- Math course of choice
- SCM science course of choice

Track A: Have your student read aloud the proverb in *Print to Cursive Proverbs,* pages 38 and 39, then carefully copy it. When he has finished the copywork, invite him to spell any word he remembers. Ask him to spell *where;* if he is unsure, allow him to look at the word. Also see if he can spell *there.*

Track B: Have your student carefully copy *Hymns in Prose Copybook,* page 18. Ask him to select a phrase from the passage to write from memory. Allow him to look at the phrase until he is sure he can spell each word in it correctly.

If your student needs more guided reading instruction, spend 15 minutes working on a lesson from the *Hymns in Prose Teacher Book.*

Math: Work on your selected math curriculum for about 20 minutes.

Science: In your SCM science course, complete the first assignment for Week 10.

TERM 1

Notes

Lesson 48

Materials Needed
- Math course of choice
- *New Friends* (Track A)
- *Hymns in Prose Copybook* (Track B)

Math: Work on your selected math curriculum for about 20 minutes.

Track A: Have your student read aloud *New Friends*, pages 159–171, "The Dumbest Thing."

Track B: Have your student carefully copy *Hymns in Prose Copybook*, page 19. Ask him to select a phrase from the passage to write from memory. Allow him to look at the phrase until he is sure he can spell each word in it correctly.

Lesson 49

Materials Needed
- *Print to Cursive Proverbs* (Track A)
- *Hymns in Prose Teacher Book* (Track B, optional)
- Math course of choice
- SCM science course of choice

Track A: Have your student read aloud the proverb at the top of *Print to Cursive Proverbs*, page 40, then complete the page.

Track B: If your student needs more guided reading instruction, spend 15 minutes working on a lesson from the *Hymns in Prose Teacher Book*.

Math: Work on your selected math curriculum for about 20 minutes.

Science: In your SCM science course, complete the second assignment for Week 10.

Lesson 50

Materials Needed
- *Print to Cursive Proverbs* (Track A)
- Math course of choice
- *Spelling Wisdom, Book 1*
- *Using Language Well, Book 1, Student Book*
- *Using Language Well, Book 1, Teacher Guide and Answer Key*
- *Journaling a Year in Nature* notebooks (optional)

Track A: Have your student complete *Print to Cursive Proverbs*, page 41.

Math: Work on your selected math curriculum for about 20 minutes.

simplycharlottemason.com

31

Notes

English: Complete *Using Language Well, Book 1,* Lesson 20.

Nature Study: Take the whole family outside for nature study.

Lesson 51

Materials Needed
- *Spelling Wisdom, Book 1*
- *Using Language Well, Book 1, Student Book*
- *Using Language Well, Book 1, Teacher Guide and Answer Key*
- Math course of choice
- *New Friends* (Track A)

English: Complete *Using Language Well, Book 1,* Lesson 21.

Math: Work on your selected math curriculum for about 20 minutes.

Track A: Have your student read aloud *New Friends,* pages 171–181, "Mrs. Wright's Gift."

Lesson 52

Materials Needed
- *Print to Cursive Proverbs* (Track A)
- *Hymns in Prose Copybook* (Track B)
- *Hymns in Prose Teacher Book* (Track B, optional)
- Math course of choice
- SCM science course of choice

Track A: Have your student read aloud the proverb in *Print to Cursive Proverbs,* pages 42 and 43, then carefully copy it. When he has finished the copywork, invite him to spell any word he remembers. Ask him to spell *green;* if he is unsure, allow him to look at the word.

Track B: Have your student carefully copy *Hymns in Prose Copybook,* page 20. Ask him to select a phrase from the passage to write from memory. Allow him to look at the phrase until he is sure he can spell each word in it correctly.

　If your student needs more guided reading instruction, spend 15 minutes working on a lesson from the *Hymns in Prose Teacher Book.*

Math: Work on your selected math curriculum for about 20 minutes.

Science: In your SCM science course, complete the first assignment for Week 11.

Lesson 53

Materials Needed
- Math course of choice
- *New Friends* (Track A)
- *Hymns in Prose Copybook* (Track B)

Math: Work on your selected math curriculum for about 20 minutes.

Track A: Have your student read aloud *New Friends,* pages 182–194, "A Fitting Name."

Track B: Have your student carefully copy *Hymns in Prose Copybook,* page 21. Ask him to select a phrase from the passage to write from memory. Allow him to look at the phrase until he is sure he can spell each word in it correctly.

Lesson 54

Materials Needed
- *Print to Cursive Proverbs* (Track A)
- *Hymns in Prose Teacher Book* (Track B, optional)
- Math course of choice
- SCM science course of choice

Track A: Have your student read aloud the proverb at the top of *Print to Cursive Proverbs,* page 44, then complete the page.

Track B: If your student needs more guided reading instruction, spend 15 minutes working on a lesson from the *Hymns in Prose Teacher Book.*

Math: Work on your selected math curriculum for about 20 minutes.

Science: In your SCM science course, complete the second assignment for Week 11.

Lesson 55

Materials Needed
- *Print to Cursive Proverbs* (Track A)
- Math course of choice
- *Spelling Wisdom, Book 1*
- *Using Language Well, Book 1, Student Book*
- *Using Language Well, Book 1, Teacher Guide and Answer Key*
- *Journaling a Year in Nature* notebooks (optional)

Track A: Have your student complete *Print to Cursive Proverbs,* page 45.

Math: Work on your selected math curriculum for about 20 minutes.

Notes

simplycharlottemason.com

Notes

English: Complete *Using Language Well, Book 1*, Lesson 22.

Nature Study: Take the whole family outside for nature study.

Lesson 56

Materials Needed
- *Spelling Wisdom, Book 1*
- *Using Language Well, Book 1, Student Book*
- *Using Language Well, Book 1, Teacher Guide and Answer Key*
- Math course of choice
- *New Friends* (Track A)

English: Complete *Using Language Well, Book 1*, Lesson 23.

Math: Work on your selected math curriculum for about 20 minutes.

Track A: Have your student read aloud *New Friends,* pages 194–204, "The Missing Cow."

Lesson 57

Materials Needed
- *Print to Cursive Proverbs* (Track A)
- *Hymns in Prose Copybook* (Track B)
- *Hymns in Prose Teacher Book* (Track B, optional)
- Math course of choice
- SCM science course of choice

Track A: Have your student read aloud the proverb in *Print to Cursive Proverbs,* page 46, then carefully copy it. When he has finished the copywork, invite him to spell any word he remembers. Ask him to spell *just;* if he is unsure, allow him to look at the word.

Track B: Have your student carefully copy *Hymns in Prose Copybook,* page 22. Ask him to select a phrase from the passage to write from memory. Allow him to look at the phrase until he is sure he can spell each word in it correctly.

   If your student needs more guided reading instruction, spend 15 minutes working on a lesson from the *Hymns in Prose Teacher Book.*

Math: Work on your selected math curriculum for about 20 minutes.

Science: In your SCM science course, complete the first assignment for Week 12.

TERM 1

Notes

Lesson 58

Materials Needed
- Math course of choice
- *New Friends* (Track A)
- *Hymns in Prose Copybook* (Track B)

Math: Work on your selected math curriculum for about 20 minutes.

Track A: Have your student read aloud *New Friends,* pages 204–215, "Better Than Ice Cream."

Track B: Have your student carefully copy *Hymns in Prose Copybook,* page 23. Ask him to select a phrase from the passage to write from memory. Allow him to look at the phrase until he is sure he can spell each word in it correctly.

Lesson 59

Materials Needed
- *Print to Cursive Proverbs,* if needed (Track A)
- *Hymns in Prose Teacher Book* (Track B, optional)
- Math course of choice
- SCM science course of choice

Track A: Use today and tomorrow to catch up on any assigned pages in *Print to Cursive Proverbs,* as needed. If desired, review these words and some of your student's selected words from previous copywork lessons: *turns, wise, false, every.* If your student is unsure about a particular word's spelling, allow him to look at the word.

Track B: If your student needs more guided reading instruction, spend 15 minutes working on a lesson from the *Hymns in Prose Teacher Book.*

Math: Work on your selected math curriculum for about 20 minutes.

Science: In your SCM science course, complete the second assignment for Week 12.

Lesson 60

Materials Needed
- *Print to Cursive Proverbs,* if needed (Track A)
- Math course of choice
- *Spelling Wisdom, Book 1*
- *Using Language Well, Book 1, Student Book*
- *Using Language Well, Book 1, Teacher Guide and Answer Key*
- *Journaling a Year in Nature* notebooks (optional)

Track A: Use today to catch up on any assigned pages in *Print to Cursive*

simplycharlottemason.com

35

TERM 1

Notes

Proverbs, as needed. If desired, review these words and more of your student's selected words from previous copywork lessons: *great, where, there, green, just.* If your student is unsure about a particular word's spelling, allow him to look at the word.

Math: Work on your selected math curriculum for about 20 minutes.

English: Complete *Using Language Well, Book 1,* Lesson 24.

Nature Study: Take the whole family outside for nature study.

Term 2

(12 weeks; 5 lessons/week)

Term 2 Resources List
- *Spelling Wisdom, Book 1*
- *Using Language Well, Book 1, Student Book*
- *Using Language Well, Book 1, Teacher Guide and Answer Key*
- Math course of choice
- Simply Charlotte Mason (SCM) science course of choice
- *Journaling a Year in Nature* notebooks (optional)

Track A
- *Print to Cursive Proverbs*
- *New Friends*
- *More New Friends*

Track B
- *Hymns in Prose for Children*
- *Hymns in Prose Teacher Book* (optional)
- *Hymns in Prose Copybook*

Weekly Schedule

	Day One	Day Two	Day Three	Day Four	Day Five
	Math (20 min.)	Math (20 min.)	Math (20 min.)	Math (20 min.)	Math (20 min.)
	(Nature Study)		Science (15–20 min.)		Science (15–20 min.)
		Spelling Wisdom & Using Language Well (10–15 min.)			Spelling Wisdom & Using Language Well (10–15 min.)
Track A	New Friends (10–15 min.)	Print to Cursive Proverbs (5–10 min.)	Print to Cursive Proverbs (5–10 min.)	New Friends (10–15 min.)	Print to Cursive Proverbs (5–10 min.)
Track B	Hymns in Prose (5–15 min.)		Hymns in Prose (5–10 min.)	Hymns in Prose (5–15 min.)	

simplycharlottemason.com

Lesson 61

Materials Needed
- Math course of choice
- *New Friends,* if needed (Track A)
- *Hymns in Prose Copybook* (Track B)
- *Hymns in Prose Teacher Book* (Track B, optional)
- *Journaling a Year in Nature* notebooks (optional)

Math: Work on your selected math curriculum for about 20 minutes.

Track A: Use today to catch up on any assigned reading in *New Friends,* as needed.

Track B: Have your student carefully copy *Hymns in Prose Copybook,* page 24. Ask him to select a phrase from the passage to write from memory. Allow him to look at the phrase until he is sure he can spell each word in it correctly.

If your student needs more guided reading instruction, spend 15 minutes working on a lesson from the *Hymns in Prose Teacher Book.*

Nature Study: Take the whole family outside for nature study.

Lesson 62

Materials Needed
- *Spelling Wisdom, Book 1*
- *Using Language Well, Book 1, Student Book*
- *Using Language Well, Book 1, Teacher Guide and Answer Key*
- Math course of choice
- *Print to Cursive Proverbs* (Track A)

English: Complete *Using Language Well, Book 1,* Lesson 25.

Math: Work on your selected math curriculum for about 20 minutes.

Track A: Have your student read aloud the proverb at the top of *Print to Cursive Proverbs,* page 47, then complete the page.

Lesson 63

Materials Needed
- SCM science course of choice
- Math course of choice
- *Print to Cursive Proverbs* (Track A)
- *Hymns in Prose Copybook* (Track B)

Science: In your SCM science course, complete the first assignment for Week 13.

Notes

Math: Work on your selected math curriculum for about 20 minutes.

Track A: Have your student complete *Print to Cursive Proverbs,* page 48.

Track B: Have your student carefully copy *Hymns in Prose Copybook,* page 25. Ask him to select a phrase from the passage to write from memory. Allow him to look at the phrase until he is sure he can spell each word in it correctly.

Lesson 64

Materials Needed
- *New Friends* (Track A)
- *Hymns in Prose Copybook* (Track B)
- *Hymns in Prose Teacher Book* (Track B, optional)
- Math course of choice

Track A: Have your student read aloud *New Friends,* pages 218–228, "Report Cards."

Track B: Have your student carefully copy *Hymns in Prose Copybook,* page 26. Ask him to select a phrase from the passage to write from memory. Allow him to look at the phrase until he is sure he can spell each word in it correctly.

If your student needs more guided reading instruction, spend 15 minutes working on a lesson from the *Hymns in Prose Teacher Book.*

Math: Work on your selected math curriculum for about 20 minutes.

Lesson 65

Materials Needed
- Math course of choice
- *Spelling Wisdom, Book 1*
- *Using Language Well, Book 1, Student Book*
- *Using Language Well, Book 1, Teacher Guide and Answer Key*
- SCM science course of choice
- *Print to Cursive Proverbs* (Track A)

Math: Work on your selected math curriculum for about 20 minutes.

English: Complete *Using Language Well, Book 1,* Lesson 26.

Science: In your SCM science course, complete the second assignment for Week 13.

Track A: Have your student read aloud the proverb in *Print to Cursive Proverbs,* pages 49 and 50, then carefully copy it. When he has finished the copywork, invite him to spell any word he remembers. Ask him to spell *known;* if he is unsure, allow him to look at the word.

Notes

Lesson 66

Materials Needed
- Math course of choice
- *New Friends* (Track A)
- *Hymns in Prose Copybook,* if needed (Track B)
- *Hymns in Prose Teacher Book* (Track B, optional)
- *Journaling a Year in Nature* notebooks (optional)

Math: Work on your selected math curriculum for about 20 minutes.

Track A: Have your student read aloud *New Friends,* pages 228–238, "Chore Time."

Track B: Use today to catch up on any assigned pages in *Hymns in Prose Copybook,* as needed. If desired, review two or three of your student's selected phrases; see if he can write each phrase correctly as you read it to him.

If your student needs more guided reading instruction, spend 15 minutes working on a lesson from the *Hymns in Prose Teacher Book.*

Nature Study: Take the whole family outside for nature study.

Lesson 67

Materials Needed
- *Spelling Wisdom, Book 1*
- *Using Language Well, Book 1, Student Book*
- *Using Language Well, Book 1, Teacher Guide and Answer Key*
- Math course of choice
- *Print to Cursive Proverbs* (Track A)

English: Complete *Using Language Well, Book 1,* Lesson 27.

Math: Work on your selected math curriculum for about 20 minutes.

Track A: Have your student read aloud the proverb at the top of *Print to Cursive Proverbs,* page 51, then complete the page.

Lesson 68

Materials Needed
- SCM science course of choice
- Math course of choice
- *Print to Cursive Proverbs* (Track A)
- *Hymns in Prose for Children* (Track B)

Science: In your SCM science course, complete the first assignment for Week 14.

Notes

Math: Work on your selected math curriculum for about 20 minutes.

Track A: Have your student complete *Print to Cursive Proverbs,* page 52.

Track B: If your student simply needs more practice reading, have him read aloud *Hymns in Prose for Children,* Hymn 5.

Lesson 69

Materials Needed
- *New Friends* (Track A)
- *Hymns in Prose Copybook* (Track B)
- *Hymns in Prose Teacher Book* (Track B, optional)
- Math course of choice

Track A: Have your student read aloud *New Friends,* pages 239–250, "One Part of Life."

Track B: Have your student carefully copy *Hymns in Prose Copybook,* page 27. Ask him to select a phrase from the passage to write from memory. Allow him to look at the phrase until he is sure he can spell each word in it correctly.

If your student needs more guided reading instruction, spend 15 minutes working on a lesson from the *Hymns in Prose Teacher Book.*

Math: Work on your selected math curriculum for about 20 minutes.

Lesson 70

Materials Needed
- Math course of choice
- *Spelling Wisdom, Book 1*
- *Using Language Well, Book 1, Student Book*
- *Using Language Well, Book 1, Teacher Guide and Answer Key*
- SCM science course of choice
- *Print to Cursive Proverbs* (Track A)

Math: Work on your selected math curriculum for about 20 minutes.

English: Complete *Using Language Well, Book 1,* Lesson 28.

Science: In your SCM science course, complete the second assignment for Week 14.

Track A: Have your student read aloud the proverb in *Print to Cursive Proverbs,* pages 53 and 54, then carefully copy it. When he has finished the copywork, invite him to spell any word he remembers. Ask him to spell *takes*; if he is unsure, allow him to look at the word.

Lesson 71

Materials Needed
- Math course of choice
- *New Friends* (Track A)
- *Hymns in Prose Copybook* (Track B)
- *Hymns in Prose Teacher Book* (Track B, optional)
- *Journaling a Year in Nature* notebooks (optional)

Math: Work on your selected math curriculum for about 20 minutes.

Track A: Have your student read aloud *New Friends,* pages 251–261, "A Trick for Dad."

Track B: Have your student carefully copy *Hymns in Prose Copybook,* page 28. Ask him to select a phrase from the passage to write from memory. Allow him to look at the phrase until he is sure he can spell each word in it correctly.

If your student needs more guided reading instruction, spend 15 minutes working on a lesson from the *Hymns in Prose Teacher Book.*

Nature Study: Take the whole family outside for nature study.

Lesson 72

Materials Needed
- *Spelling Wisdom, Book 1*
- *Using Language Well, Book 1, Student Book*
- *Using Language Well, Book 1, Teacher Guide and Answer Key*
- Math course of choice
- *Print to Cursive Proverbs* (Track A)

English: Complete *Using Language Well, Book 1,* Lesson 29.

Math: Work on your selected math curriculum for about 20 minutes.

Track A: Have your student read aloud the proverb at the top of *Print to Cursive Proverbs,* page 55, then complete the page.

Lesson 73

Materials Needed
- SCM science course of choice
- Math course of choice
- *Print to Cursive Proverbs* (Track A)
- *Hymns in Prose Copybook* (Track B)

Science: In your SCM science course, complete the first assignment for Week 15.

Notes

Math: Work on your selected math curriculum for about 20 minutes.

Track A: Have your student complete *Print to Cursive Proverbs,* page 56.

Track B: Have your student carefully copy *Hymns in Prose Copybook,* page 29. Ask him to select a phrase from the passage to write from memory. Allow him to look at the phrase until he is sure he can spell each word in it correctly.

Lesson 74

Materials Needed
- *New Friends* (Track A)
- *Hymns in Prose Copybook* (Track B)
- *Hymns in Prose Teacher Book* (Track B, optional)
- Math course of choice

Track A: Have your student read aloud *New Friends,* pages 261–268, "A Glass of Warm Water."

Track B: Have your student carefully copy *Hymns in Prose Copybook,* page 30. Ask him to select a phrase from the passage to write from memory. Allow him to look at the phrase until he is sure he can spell each word in it correctly.

If your student needs more guided reading instruction, spend 15 minutes working on a lesson from the *Hymns in Prose Teacher Book.*

Math: Work on your selected math curriculum for about 20 minutes.

Reminder: Get More New Friends *for lesson 84 for Track A.*

Lesson 75

Materials Needed
- Math course of choice
- *Spelling Wisdom, Book 1*
- *Using Language Well, Book 1, Student Book*
- *Using Language Well, Book 1, Teacher Guide and Answer Key*
- SCM science course of choice
- *Print to Cursive Proverbs* (Track A)

Math: Work on your selected math curriculum for about 20 minutes.

English: Complete *Using Language Well, Book 1,* Lesson 30.

Science: In your SCM science course, complete the second assignment for Week 15.

Track A: Have your student read aloud the proverb in *Print to Cursive Proverbs,* pages 57 and 58, then carefully copy it. When he has finished the copywork, invite him to spell any word he remembers. Ask him to spell *opens*; if he is unsure, allow him to look at the word.

Lesson 76

Materials Needed
- Math course of choice
- *New Friends* (Track A)
- *Hymns in Prose Copybook* (Track B)
- *Hymns in Prose Teacher Book* (Track B, optional)
- *Journaling a Year in Nature* notebooks (optional)

Math: Work on your selected math curriculum for about 20 minutes.

Track A: Have your student read aloud *New Friends,* pages 268–279, "Bitternut Hickory."

Track B: Have your student carefully copy *Hymns in Prose Copybook,* page 31. Ask him to select a phrase from the passage to write from memory. Allow him to look at the phrase until he is sure he can spell each word in it correctly.

If your student needs more guided reading instruction, spend 15 minutes working on a lesson from the *Hymns in Prose Teacher Book.*

Nature Study: Take the whole family outside for nature study.

Lesson 77

Materials Needed
- *Spelling Wisdom, Book 1*
- *Using Language Well, Book 1, Student Book*
- *Using Language Well, Book 1, Teacher Guide and Answer Key*
- Math course of choice
- *Print to Cursive Proverbs* (Track A)

English: Complete *Using Language Well, Book 1,* Lesson 31.

Math: Work on your selected math curriculum for about 20 minutes.

Track A: Have your student read aloud the proverb at the top of *Print to Cursive Proverbs,* page 59, then complete the page.

Lesson 78

Materials Needed
- SCM science course of choice
- Math course of choice
- *Print to Cursive Proverbs* (Track A)

Notes

- *Hymns in Prose Copybook* (Track B)

Science: In your SCM science course, complete the first assignment for Week 16.

Math: Work on your selected math curriculum for about 20 minutes.

Track A: Have your student complete *Print to Cursive Proverbs,* page 60.

Track B: Have your student carefully copy *Hymns in Prose Copybook,* page 32. Ask him to select a phrase from the passage to write from memory. Allow him to look at the phrase until he is sure he can spell each word in it correctly.

Lesson 79

Materials Needed
- *New Friends,* if needed (Track A)
- *Hymns in Prose Copybook* (Track B)
- *Hymns in Prose Teacher Book* (Track B, optional)
- Math course of choice

Track A: Use today and lesson 81 to catch up on any assigned reading in *New Friends,* as needed.

Track B: Have your student carefully copy *Hymns in Prose Copybook,* page 33. Ask him to select a phrase from the passage to write from memory. Allow him to look at the phrase until he is sure he can spell each word in it correctly.

If your student needs more guided reading instruction, spend 15 minutes working on a lesson from the *Hymns in Prose Teacher Book.*

Math: Work on your selected math curriculum for about 20 minutes.

Lesson 80

Materials Needed
- Math course of choice
- *Spelling Wisdom, Book 1*
- *Using Language Well, Book 1, Student Book*
- *Using Language Well, Book 1, Teacher Guide and Answer Key*
- SCM science course of choice
- *Print to Cursive Proverbs,* if needed (Track A)

Math: Work on your selected math curriculum for about 20 minutes.

English: Complete *Using Language Well, Book 1,* Lesson 32.

Science: In your SCM science course, complete the second assignment for Week 16.

Track A: Use today to catch up on any assigned pages in *Print to Cursive Proverbs,* as needed. If desired, review these words and your student's selected words from previous copywork lessons: *known, takes, opens.* If your student is unsure about a particular word's spelling, allow him to look at the word.

Lesson 81

Materials Needed
- Math course of choice
- *New Friends,* if needed (Track A)
- *Hymns in Prose Copybook* (Track B)
- *Hymns in Prose Teacher Book* (Track B, optional)
- *Journaling a Year in Nature* notebooks (optional)

Math: Work on your selected math curriculum for about 20 minutes.

Track A: Use today to catch up on any assigned reading in *New Friends,* as needed.

Track B: Have your student carefully copy *Hymns in Prose Copybook,* page 34. Ask him to select a phrase from the passage to write from memory. Allow him to look at the phrase until he is sure he can spell each word in it correctly.

If your student needs more guided reading instruction, spend 15 minutes working on a lesson from the *Hymns in Prose Teacher Book.*

Nature Study: Take the whole family outside for nature study.

Lesson 82

Materials Needed
- *Spelling Wisdom, Book 1*
- *Using Language Well, Book 1, Student Book*
- *Using Language Well, Book 1, Teacher Guide and Answer Key*
- Math course of choice
- *Print to Cursive Proverbs* (Track A)

English: Complete *Using Language Well, Book 1,* Lesson 33.

Math: Work on your selected math curriculum for about 20 minutes.

Track A: Have your student read aloud the proverb in *Print to Cursive Proverbs,* pages 61 and 62, then carefully copy it. When he has finished the copywork, invite him to spell any word he remembers. Ask him to spell *does*; if he is unsure, allow him to look at the word.

Notes

Lesson 83

Materials Needed
- SCM science course of choice
- Math course of choice
- *Print to Cursive Proverbs* (Track A)
- *Hymns in Prose Copybook* (Track B)

Science: In your SCM science course, complete the first assignment for Week 17.

Math: Work on your selected math curriculum for about 20 minutes.

Track A: Have your student read aloud the proverb at the top of *Print to Cursive Proverbs,* page 63, then complete the page.

Track B: Have your student carefully copy *Hymns in Prose Copybook,* page 35. Ask him to select a phrase from the passage to write from memory. Allow him to look at the phrase until he is sure he can spell each word in it correctly.

Lesson 84

Materials Needed
- *More New Friends* (Track A)
- *Hymns in Prose Copybook* (Track B)
- *Hymns in Prose Teacher Book* (Track B, optional)
- Math course of choice

Track A: Have your student read aloud *More New Friends,* pages 6–10, "An Exciting Day."

Track B: Have your student carefully copy *Hymns in Prose Copybook,* page 36. Ask him to select a phrase from the passage to write from memory. Allow him to look at the phrase until he is sure he can spell each word in it correctly.
    If your student needs more guided reading instruction, spend 15 minutes working on a lesson from the *Hymns in Prose Teacher Book*.

Math: Work on your selected math curriculum for about 20 minutes.

Lesson 85

Materials Needed
- Math course of choice
- *Spelling Wisdom, Book 1*
- *Using Language Well, Book 1, Student Book*
- *Using Language Well, Book 1, Teacher Guide and Answer Key*
- SCM science course of choice
- *Print to Cursive Proverbs* (Track A)

Math: Work on your selected math curriculum for about 20 minutes.

English: Complete *Using Language Well, Book 1,* Lesson 34.

Science: In your SCM science course, complete the second assignment for Week 17.

Track A: Have your student complete *Print to Cursive Proverbs,* page 64.

Lesson 86

Materials Needed
- Math course of choice
- *More New Friends* (Track A)
- *Hymns in Prose Copybook* (Track B)
- *Hymns in Prose Teacher Book* (Track B, optional)
- *Journaling a Year in Nature* notebooks (optional)

Math: Work on your selected math curriculum for about 20 minutes.

Track A: Have your student read aloud *More New Friends,* pages 10–20, "Tusky, An African Elephant."

Track B: Have your student carefully copy *Hymns in Prose Copybook,* page 37. Ask him to select a phrase from the passage to write from memory. Allow him to look at the phrase until he is sure he can spell each word in it correctly.

If your student needs more guided reading instruction, spend 15 minutes working on a lesson from the *Hymns in Prose Teacher Book.*

Nature Study: Take the whole family outside for nature study.

Lesson 87

Materials Needed
- *Spelling Wisdom, Book 1*
- *Using Language Well, Book 1, Student Book*
- *Using Language Well, Book 1, Teacher Guide and Answer Key*
- Math course of choice
- *Print to Cursive Proverbs* (Track A)

English: Complete *Using Language Well, Book 1,* Lesson 35.

Math: Work on your selected math curriculum for about 20 minutes.

Track A: Have your student read aloud the proverb in *Print to Cursive Proverbs,* pages 65 and 66, then carefully copy it. When he has finished the copywork, invite him to spell any word he remembers. Ask him to spell *heart*; if he is unsure, allow him to look at the word.

Notes

Lesson 88

Materials Needed
- SCM science course of choice
- Math course of choice
- *Print to Cursive Proverbs* (Track A)
- *Hymns in Prose Copybook* (Track B)

Science: In your SCM science course, complete the first assignment for Week 18.

Math: Work on your selected math curriculum for about 20 minutes.

Track A: Have your student read aloud the proverb at the top of *Print to Cursive Proverbs*, page 67, then complete the page.

Track B: Have your student carefully copy *Hymns in Prose Copybook*, page 38. Ask him to select a phrase from the passage to write from memory. Allow him to look at the phrase until he is sure he can spell each word in it correctly.

Lesson 89

Materials Needed
- *More New Friends* (Track A)
- *Hymns in Prose Copybook* (Track B)
- *Hymns in Prose Teacher Book* (Track B, optional)
- Math course of choice

Track A: Have your student read aloud *More New Friends*, pages 20–32, "King of the Mountain."

Track B: Have your student carefully copy *Hymns in Prose Copybook*, pages 39 and 40. Ask him to select a phrase from the passage to write from memory. Allow him to look at the phrase until he is sure he can spell each word in it correctly.

If your student needs more guided reading instruction, spend 15 minutes working on a lesson from the *Hymns in Prose Teacher Book*.

Math: Work on your selected math curriculum for about 20 minutes.

Lesson 90

Materials Needed
- Math course of choice
- *Spelling Wisdom, Book 1*
- *Using Language Well, Book 1, Student Book*
- *Using Language Well, Book 1, Teacher Guide and Answer Key*
- SCM science course of choice
- *Print to Cursive Proverbs* (Track A)

Math: Work on your selected math curriculum for about 20 minutes.

English: Complete *Using Language Well, Book 1,* Lesson 36.

Science: In your SCM science course, complete the second assignment for Week 18.

Track A: Have your student complete *Print to Cursive Proverbs,* page 68.

Lesson 91

Materials Needed
- Math course of choice
- *More New Friends* (Track A)
- *Hymns in Prose for Children* (Track B)
- *Hymns in Prose Copybook,* if needed (Track B)
- *Hymns in Prose Teacher Book* (Track B, optional)
- *Journaling a Year in Nature* notebooks (optional)

Math: Work on your selected math curriculum for about 20 minutes.

Track A: Have your student read aloud *More New Friends,* pages 32–42, "Alice, the Alligator."

Track B: Use today to catch up on any assigned pages in *Hymns in Prose Copybook,* as needed. If desired, review two or three of your student's selected phrases; see if he can write each phrase correctly as you read it to him.
   If your student needs more guided reading instruction, spend 15 minutes working on a lesson from the *Hymns in Prose Teacher Book.*
   If he simply needs more practice reading, have him read aloud *Hymns in Prose for Children,* Hymn 6.

Nature Study: Take the whole family outside for nature study.

Lesson 92

Materials Needed
- *Spelling Wisdom, Book 1*
- *Using Language Well, Book 1, Student Book*
- *Using Language Well, Book 1, Teacher Guide and Answer Key*
- Math course of choice
- *Print to Cursive Proverbs* (Track A)

English: Complete *Using Language Well, Book 1,* Lesson 37.

Math: Work on your selected math curriculum for about 20 minutes.

Track A: Have your student read aloud the proverb in *Print to Cursive Proverbs,* pages 69 and 70, then carefully copy it. When he has finished the copywork,

Notes

invite him to spell any word he remembers. Ask him to spell *give*; if he is unsure, allow him to look at the word.

Lesson 93

Materials Needed
- SCM science course of choice
- Math course of choice
- *Print to Cursive Proverbs* (Track A)
- *Hymns in Prose for Children* (Track B)

Science: In your SCM science course, complete the first assignment for Week 19.

Math: Work on your selected math curriculum for about 20 minutes.

Track A: Have your student read aloud the proverb at the top of *Print to Cursive Proverbs*, page 71, then complete the page.

Track B: If your student simply needs more practice reading, have him read aloud *Hymns in Prose for Children*, Hymn 7.

Lesson 94

Materials Needed
- *More New Friends* (Track A)
- *Hymns in Prose for Children* (Track B)
- *Hymns in Prose Teacher Book* (Track B, optional)
- Math course of choice

Track A: Have your student read aloud *More New Friends*, pages 42–50, "Shaggy, the Buffalo."

Track B: If your student needs more guided reading instruction, spend 15 minutes working on a lesson from the *Hymns in Prose Teacher Book*.
   If he simply needs more practice reading, have your student read aloud *Hymns in Prose for Children*, Hymn 8.

Math: Work on your selected math curriculum for about 20 minutes.

Lesson 95

Materials Needed
- Math course of choice
- *Spelling Wisdom, Book 1*
- *Using Language Well, Book 1, Student Book*
- *Using Language Well, Book 1, Teacher Guide and Answer Key*
- SCM science course of choice

- *Print to Cursive Proverbs* (Track A)

Math: Work on your selected math curriculum for about 20 minutes.

English: Complete *Using Language Well, Book 1,* Lesson 38.

Science: In your SCM science course, complete the second assignment for Week 19.

Track A: Have your student complete *Print to Cursive Proverbs,* page 72.

Lesson 96

Materials Needed
- Math course of choice
- *More New Friends,* if needed (Track A)
- *Hymns in Prose Teacher Book* (Track B, optional)
- *Hymns in Prose Copybook* (Track B)
- *Journaling a Year in Nature* notebooks (optional)

Math: Work on your selected math curriculum for about 20 minutes.

Track A: Use today to catch up on any assigned reading in *More New Friends,* as needed.

Track B: Have your student carefully copy *Hymns in Prose Copybook,* page 41. Ask him to select a phrase from the passage to write from memory. Allow him to look at the phrase until he is sure he can spell each word in it correctly.

If your student needs more guided reading instruction, spend 15 minutes working on a lesson from the *Hymns in Prose Teacher Book.*

Nature Study: Take the whole family outside for nature study.

Lesson 97

Materials Needed
- *Spelling Wisdom, Book 1*
- *Using Language Well, Book 1, Student Book*
- *Using Language Well, Book 1, Teacher Guide and Answer Key*
- Math course of choice
- *Print to Cursive Proverbs,* if needed (Track A)

English: Complete *Using Language Well, Book 1,* Lesson 39.

Math: Work on your selected math curriculum for about 20 minutes.

Track A: Use today to catch up on any assigned pages in *Print to Cursive Proverbs,* as needed. If desired, review these words and your student's selected words from previous copywork lessons: *does, heart, give.* If your student is

Notes

unsure about a particular word's spelling, allow him to look at the word.

Lesson 98

Materials Needed
- SCM science course of choice
- Math course of choice
- *Print to Cursive Proverbs* (Track A)
- *Hymns in Prose Copybook* (Track B)

Science: In your SCM science course, complete the first assignment for Week 20.

Math: Work on your selected math curriculum for about 20 minutes.

Track A: Have your student read aloud the proverb in *Print to Cursive Proverbs,* pages 73 and 74, then carefully copy it. When he has finished the copywork, invite him to spell any word he remembers. Ask him to spell *water*; if he is unsure, allow him to look at the word.

Track B: Have your student carefully copy *Hymns in Prose Copybook,* page 42. Ask him to select a phrase from the passage to write from memory. Allow him to look at the phrase until he is sure he can spell each word in it correctly.

Lesson 99

Materials Needed
- *More New Friends* (Track A)
- *Hymns in Prose Copybook* (Track B)
- *Hymns in Prose Teacher Book* (Track B, optional)
- Math course of choice

Track A: Have your student read aloud *More New Friends,* pages 52–64, "The Snaky Bridge."

Track B: Have your student carefully copy *Hymns in Prose Copybook,* page 43. Ask him to select a phrase from the passage to write from memory. Allow him to look at the phrase until he is sure he can spell each word in it correctly.

If your student needs more guided reading instruction, spend 15 minutes working on a lesson from the *Hymns in Prose Teacher Book.*

Math: Work on your selected math curriculum for about 20 minutes.

Lesson 100

Materials Needed
- Math course of choice
- *Spelling Wisdom, Book 1*

Notes

- *Using Language Well, Book 1, Student Book*
- *Using Language Well, Book 1, Teacher Guide and Answer Key*
- SCM science course of choice
- *Print to Cursive Proverbs* (Track A)

Math: Work on your selected math curriculum for about 20 minutes.

English: Complete *Using Language Well, Book 1,* Lesson 40.

Science: In your SCM science course, complete the second assignment for Week 20.

Track A: Have your student read aloud the proverb at the top of *Print to Cursive Proverbs,* page 75, then complete the page.

Lesson 101

Materials Needed
- Math course of choice
- *More New Friends* (Track A)
- *Hymns in Prose Copybook* (Track B)
- *Hymns in Prose Teacher Book* (Track B, optional)
- *Journaling a Year in Nature* notebooks (optional)

Math: Work on your selected math curriculum for about 20 minutes.

Track A: Have your student read aloud *More New Friends,* pages 64–76, "Crossing the Bridge."

Track B: Have your student carefully copy *Hymns in Prose Copybook,* page 44. Ask him to select a phrase from the passage to write from memory. Allow him to look at the phrase until he is sure he can spell each word in it correctly.

If your student needs more guided reading instruction, spend 15 minutes working on a lesson from the *Hymns in Prose Teacher Book.*

Nature Study: Take the whole family outside for nature study.

Lesson 102

Materials Needed
- *Spelling Wisdom, Book 1*
- *Using Language Well, Book 1, Student Book*
- *Using Language Well, Book 1, Teacher Guide and Answer Key*
- Math course of choice
- *Print to Cursive Proverbs* (Track A)

English: Complete *Using Language Well, Book 1,* Lesson 41.

Math: Work on your selected math curriculum for about 20 minutes.

Notes

Track A: Have your student complete *Print to Cursive Proverbs,* page 76. When he has finished the copywork, invite him to spell any word he remembers. Ask him to spell *quick*; if he is unsure, allow him to look at the word.

Lesson 103

Materials Needed
- SCM science course of choice
- Math course of choice
- *Print to Cursive Proverbs* (Track A)
- *Hymns in Prose Copybook* (Track B)

Science: In your SCM science course, complete the first assignment for Week 21.

Math: Work on your selected math curriculum for about 20 minutes.

Track A: Have your student read aloud the proverb at the top of *Print to Cursive Proverbs,* page 77, then complete pages 77 and 78.

Track B: Have your student carefully copy *Hymns in Prose Copybook,* page 45. Ask him to select a phrase from the passage to write from memory. Allow him to look at the phrase until he is sure he can spell each word in it correctly.

Lesson 104

Materials Needed
- *More New Friends* (Track A)
- *Hymns in Prose Copybook* (Track B)
- *Hymns in Prose Teacher Book* (Track B, optional)
- Math course of choice

Track A: Have your student read aloud *More New Friends,* pages 77–88, "Busy Days."

Track B: Have your student carefully copy *Hymns in Prose Copybook,* page 46. Ask him to select a phrase from the passage to write from memory. Allow him to look at the phrase until he is sure he can spell each word in it correctly.
    If your student needs more guided reading instruction, spend 15 minutes working on a lesson from the *Hymns in Prose Teacher Book.*

Math: Work on your selected math curriculum for about 20 minutes.

Lesson 105

Materials Needed
- Math course of choice
- *Spelling Wisdom, Book 1*

Notes

- *Using Language Well, Book 1, Student Book*
- *Using Language Well, Book 1, Teacher Guide and Answer Key*
- SCM science course of choice
- *Print to Cursive Proverbs* (Track A)

Math: Work on your selected math curriculum for about 20 minutes.

English: Complete *Using Language Well, Book 1,* Lesson 42.

Science: In your SCM science course, complete the second assignment for Week 21.

Track A: Have your student complete *Print to Cursive Proverbs,* page 79. When he has finished the copywork, invite him to spell any word he remembers. Ask him to spell *wind*; if he is unsure, allow him to look at the word.

Lesson 106

Materials Needed
- Math course of choice
- *More New Friends* (Track A)
- *Hymns in Prose Copybook* (Track B)
- *Hymns in Prose Teacher Book* (Track B, optional)
- *Journaling a Year in Nature* notebooks (optional)

Math: Work on your selected math curriculum for about 20 minutes.

Track A: Have your student read aloud *More New Friends,* pages 88–95, "Two Thankful Girls."

Track B: Have your student carefully copy *Hymns in Prose Copybook,* page 47. Ask him to select a phrase from the passage to write from memory. Allow him to look at the phrase until he is sure he can spell each word in it correctly.

If your student needs more guided reading instruction, spend 15 minutes working on a lesson from the *Hymns in Prose Teacher Book.*

Nature Study: Take the whole family outside for nature study.

Lesson 107

Materials Needed
- *Spelling Wisdom, Book 1*
- *Using Language Well, Book 1, Student Book*
- *Using Language Well, Book 1, Teacher Guide and Answer Key*
- Math course of choice
- *Print to Cursive Proverbs* (Track A)

English: Complete *Using Language Well, Book 1,* Lesson 43.

Notes

Math: Work on your selected math curriculum for about 20 minutes.

Track A: Have your student read aloud the proverb at the top of *Print to Cursive Proverbs,* page 80, then copy the first phrase: "Do not rejoice when your enemy falls,". When he has finished the copywork, invite him to spell any word he remembers. Ask him to spell *when*; if he is unsure, allow him to look at the word.

Lesson 108

Materials Needed
- SCM science course of choice
- Math course of choice
- *Print to Cursive Proverbs* (Track A)
- *Hymns in Prose Copybook* (Track B)

Science: In your SCM science course, complete the first assignment for Week 22.

Math: Work on your selected math curriculum for about 20 minutes.

Track A: Have your student read aloud the proverb at the top of *Print to Cursive Proverbs,* page 80, then copy the rest of the proverb on pages 81 and the top of 82.

Track B: Have your student carefully copy *Hymns in Prose Copybook,* page 48. Ask him to select a phrase from the passage to write from memory. Allow him to look at the phrase until he is sure he can spell each word in it correctly.

Lesson 109

Materials Needed
- *More New Friends* (Track A)
- *Hymns in Prose Copybook* (Track B)
- *Hymns in Prose Teacher Book* (Track B, optional)
- Math course of choice

Track A: Have your student read aloud *More New Friends,* pages 96–105, "Vacation for Mother."

Track B: Have your student carefully copy *Hymns in Prose Copybook,* page 49. Ask him to select a phrase from the passage to write from memory. Allow him to look at the phrase until he is sure he can spell each word in it correctly.
   If your student needs more guided reading instruction, spend 15 minutes working on a lesson from the *Hymns in Prose Teacher Book.*

Math: Work on your selected math curriculum for about 20 minutes.

Lesson 110

Materials Needed
- Math course of choice
- *Spelling Wisdom, Book 1*
- *Using Language Well, Book 1, Student Book*
- *Using Language Well, Book 1, Teacher Guide and Answer Key*
- SCM science course of choice
- *Print to Cursive Proverbs* (Track A)

Math: Work on your selected math curriculum for about 20 minutes.

English: Complete *Using Language Well, Book 1,* Lesson 44.

Science: In your SCM science course, complete the second assignment for Week 22.

Track A: Have your student complete the rest of *Print to Cursive Proverbs,* page 82. When he has finished the copywork, invite him to spell any word he remembers. Ask him to spell *farm*; if he is unsure, allow him to look at the word.

Lesson 111

Materials Needed
- Math course of choice
- *More New Friends* (Track A)
- *Hymns in Prose Copybook* (Track B)
- *Hymns in Prose Teacher Book* (Track B, optional)
- *Journaling a Year in Nature* notebooks (optional)

Math: Work on your selected math curriculum for about 20 minutes.

Track A: Have your student read aloud *More New Friends,* pages 105–116, "A Happy, Busy Day."

Track B: Have your student carefully copy *Hymns in Prose Copybook,* page 50. Ask him to select a phrase from the passage to write from memory. Allow him to look at the phrase until he is sure he can spell each word in it correctly.

If your student needs more guided reading instruction, spend 15 minutes working on a lesson from the *Hymns in Prose Teacher Book.*

Nature Study: Take the whole family outside for nature study.

Lesson 112

Materials Needed
- *Spelling Wisdom, Book 1*
- *Using Language Well, Book 1, Student Book*
- *Using Language Well, Book 1, Teacher Guide and Answer Key*

TERM

Notes

- Math course of choice
- *Print to Cursive Proverbs* (Track A)

English: Complete *Using Language Well, Book 1,* Lesson 45.

Math: Work on your selected math curriculum for about 20 minutes.

Track A: Have your student read aloud the proverb at the top of *Print to Cursive Proverbs,* page 83, then copy the first part: "The reward for humility and fear of the Lord."

Lesson 113

Materials Needed
- SCM science course of choice
- Math course of choice
- *Print to Cursive Proverbs* (Track A)
- *Hymns in Prose Copybook* (Track B)

Science: In your SCM science course, complete the first assignment for Week 23.

Math: Work on your selected math curriculum for about 20 minutes.

Track A: Have your student read aloud the proverb at the top of *Print to Cursive Proverbs,* page 83, then copy the rest of the proverb on pages 84 and the top of 85. When he has finished the copywork, invite him to spell any word he remembers. Ask him to spell *riches*; if he is unsure, allow him to look at the word.

Track B: Have your student carefully copy *Hymns in Prose Copybook,* page 51. Ask him to select a phrase from the passage to write from memory. Allow him to look at the phrase until he is sure he can spell each word in it correctly.

Lesson 114

Materials Needed
- *More New Friends,* if needed (Track A)
- *Hymns in Prose Copybook* (Track B)
- *Hymns in Prose Teacher Book* (Track B, optional)
- Math course of choice

Track A: Use today and lessons 116 and 119 to catch up on any assigned reading in *More New Friends,* as needed.

Track B: Have your student carefully copy *Hymns in Prose Copybook,* page 52. Ask him to select a phrase from the passage to write from memory. Allow him to look at the phrase until he is sure he can spell each word in it correctly.

If your student needs more guided reading instruction, spend 15 minutes working on a lesson from the *Hymns in Prose Teacher Book*.

Math: Work on your selected math curriculum for about 20 minutes.

Lesson 115

Materials Needed
- Math course of choice
- *Spelling Wisdom, Book 1*
- *Using Language Well, Book 1, Student Book*
- *Using Language Well, Book 1, Teacher Guide and Answer Key*
- SCM science course of choice
- *Print to Cursive Proverbs* (Track A)

Math: Work on your selected math curriculum for about 20 minutes.

English: Complete *Using Language Well, Book 1,* Lesson 46.

Science: In your SCM science course, complete the second assignment for Week 23.

Track A: Have your student complete the rest of *Print to Cursive Proverbs,* page 85. When he has finished the copywork, invite him to spell any word he remembers. Ask him to spell *why*; if he is unsure, allow him to look at the word.

Lesson 116

Materials Needed
- Math course of choice
- *More New Friends,* if needed (Track A)
- *Hymns in Prose Copybook* (Track B)
- *Hymns in Prose Teacher Book* (Track B, optional)
- *Journaling a Year in Nature* notebooks (optional)

Math: Work on your selected math curriculum for about 20 minutes.

Track A: Use today and lesson 119 to catch up on any assigned reading in *More New Friends,* as needed.

Track B: Have your student carefully copy *Hymns in Prose Copybook,* page 53. Ask him to select a phrase from the passage to write from memory. Allow him to look at the phrase until he is sure he can spell each word in it correctly.

If your student needs more guided reading instruction, spend 15 minutes working on a lesson from the *Hymns in Prose Teacher Book.*

Nature Study: Take the whole family outside for nature study.

Notes

Lesson 117

Materials Needed
- *Spelling Wisdom, Book 1*
- *Using Language Well, Book 1, Student Book*
- *Using Language Well, Book 1, Teacher Guide and Answer Key*
- Math course of choice
- *Print to Cursive Proverbs* (Track A)

English: Complete *Using Language Well, Book 1,* Lesson 47.

Math: Work on your selected math curriculum for about 20 minutes.

Track A: Have your student read aloud the proverb at the top of *Print to Cursive Proverbs,* page 86, then copy the first part: "Whoever is slow to anger has great understanding,".

Lesson 118

Materials Needed
- SCM science course of choice
- Math course of choice
- *Print to Cursive Proverbs* (Track A)
- *Hymns in Prose Copybook* (Track B)

Science: In your SCM science course, complete the first assignment for Week 24.

Math: Work on your selected math curriculum for about 20 minutes.

Track A: Have your student read aloud the proverb at the top of *Print to Cursive Proverbs,* page 86, then copy the rest of pages 87 and 88. When he has finished the copywork, invite him to spell any word he remembers. Ask him to spell *who*; if he is unsure, allow him to look at the word.

Track B: Have your student carefully copy *Hymns in Prose Copybook,* page 54. Ask him to select a phrase from the passage to write from memory. Allow him to look at the phrase until he is sure he can spell each word in it correctly.

Lesson 119

Materials Needed
- *More New Friends,* if needed (Track A)
- *Hymns in Prose Copybook* (Track B)
- *Hymns in Prose Teacher Book* (Track B, optional)
- Math course of choice

Track A: Use today to catch up on any assigned reading in *More New Friends,* as needed.

Track B: Have your student carefully copy *Hymns in Prose Copybook,* pages 55 and 56. Ask him to select a phrase from the passage to write from memory. Allow him to look at the phrase until he is sure he can spell each word in it correctly.

If your student needs more guided reading instruction, spend 15 minutes working on a lesson from the *Hymns in Prose Teacher Book.*

Math: Work on your selected math curriculum for about 20 minutes.

Lesson 120

Materials Needed
- Math course of choice
- *Spelling Wisdom, Book 1*
- *Using Language Well, Book 1, Student Book*
- *Using Language Well, Book 1, Teacher Guide and Answer Key*
- SCM science course of choice
- *Print to Cursive Proverbs,* if needed (Track A)

Math: Work on your selected math curriculum for about 20 minutes.

English: Complete *Using Language Well, Book 1,* Lesson 48.

Science: In your SCM science course, complete the second assignment for Week 24.

Track A: Use today to catch up on any assigned pages in *Print to Cursive Proverbs,* as needed. If desired, review these words and your student's selected words from previous copywork lessons: *water, quick, wind, when, farm, riches, why, who.* If your student is unsure about a particular word's spelling, allow him to look at the word.

Notes

Term 3

(12 weeks; 5 lessons/week)

Term 3 Resources List

- *Spelling Wisdom, Book 1*
- *Using Language Well, Book 1, Student Book*
- *Using Language Well, Book 1, Teacher Guide and Answer Key*
- Math course of choice
- Simply Charlotte Mason (SCM) science course of choice
- *Journaling a Year in Nature* notebooks (optional)

Track A
- *Print to Cursive Proverbs*
- *More New Friends*

Track B
- *Hymns in Prose for Children*
- *Hymns in Prose Teacher Book* (optional)
- *Hymns in Prose Copybook*

Weekly Schedule

	Day One	Day Two	Day Three	Day Four	Day Five
	Math (20 min.)	Math (20 min.)	Math (20 min.)	Math (20 min.)	Math (20 min.)
		Science (15–20 min.)		(Nature Study)	Science (15–20 min.)
	Spelling Wisdom & Using Language Well (10–15 min.)			Spelling Wisdom & Using Language Well (10–15 min.)	
Track A	More New Friends (10–15 min.)	Print to Cursive Proverbs (5–10 min.)	More New Friends (10–15 min.)		Print to Cursive Proverbs (5–10 min.)
Track B		Hymns in Prose (5–10 min.)	Hymns in Prose (5–15 min.)		Hymns in Prose (5–10 min.)

TERM

Notes

Lesson 121

Materials Needed
- *More New Friends* (Track A)
- Math course of choice
- *Spelling Wisdom, Book 1*
- *Using Language Well, Book 1, Student Book*
- *Using Language Well, Book 1, Teacher Guide and Answer Key*

Track A: Have your student read aloud *More New Friends,* pages 118–127, "Slow Feet."

Math: Work on your selected math curriculum for about 20 minutes.

English: Complete *Using Language Well, Book 1,* Lesson 49.

Lesson 122

Materials Needed
- SCM science course of choice
- Math course of choice
- *Print to Cursive Proverbs* (Track A)
- *Hymns in Prose for Children* (Track B)

Science: In your SCM science course, complete the first assignment for Week 25.

Math: Work on your selected math curriculum for about 20 minutes.

Track A: Have your student read aloud the proverb at the top of *Print to Cursive Proverbs,* page 89, then copy the first part: "A tranquil heart gives life to the flesh,".

Track B: If your student simply needs more practice reading, have him read aloud *Hymns in Prose for Children,* Hymn 9.

Lesson 123

Materials Needed
- *More New Friends* (Track A)
- *Hymns in Prose for Children* (Track B)
- *Hymns in Prose Teacher Book* (Track B, optional)
- Math course of choice

Track A: Have your student read aloud *More New Friends,* pages 127–142, "Singing Wheels."

Track B: If your student needs more guided reading instruction, spend 15 minutes working on a lesson from the *Hymns in Prose Teacher Book*.

Notes

If he simply needs more practice reading, have your student read aloud *Hymns in Prose for Children*, Hymn 10.

Math: Work on your selected math curriculum for about 20 minutes.

Lesson 124

Materials Needed
- Math course of choice
- *Spelling Wisdom, Book 1*
- *Using Language Well, Book 1, Student Book*
- *Using Language Well, Book 1, Teacher Guide and Answer Key*
- *Journaling a Year in Nature* notebooks (optional)

Math: Work on your selected math curriculum for about 20 minutes.

English: Complete *Using Language Well, Book 1*, Lesson 50.

Nature Study: Take the whole family outside for nature study.

Lesson 125

Materials Needed
- *Print to Cursive Proverbs* (Track A)
- *Hymns in Prose Copybook* (Track B)
- Math course of choice
- SCM science course of choice

Track A: Have your student read aloud the proverb at the top of *Print to Cursive Proverbs*, page 89, then copy the rest of page 90. When he has finished the copywork, invite him to spell any word he remembers. Ask him to spell *bones*; if he is unsure, allow him to look at the word.

Track B: Have your student carefully copy *Hymns in Prose Copybook*, page 57. Ask him to select a phrase from the passage to write from memory. Allow him to look at the phrase until he is sure he can spell each word in it correctly.

Math: Work on your selected math curriculum for about 20 minutes.

Science: In your SCM science course, complete the second assignment for Week 25.

Lesson 126

Materials Needed
- *More New Friends* (Track A)
- Math course of choice
- *Spelling Wisdom, Book 1*

TERM

Notes

- *Using Language Well, Book 1, Student Book*
- *Using Language Well, Book 1, Teacher Guide and Answer Key*

Track A: Have your student read aloud *More New Friends,* pages 142–151, "The Lost Billfold."

Math: Work on your selected math curriculum for about 20 minutes.

English: Complete *Using Language Well, Book 1,* Lesson 51.

Lesson 127

Materials Needed
- SCM science course of choice
- Math course of choice
- *Print to Cursive Proverbs* (Track A)
- *Hymns in Prose Copybook* (Track B)

Science: In your SCM science course, complete the first assignment for Week 26.

Math: Work on your selected math curriculum for about 20 minutes.

Track A: Have your student complete *Print to Cursive Proverbs,* page 91. When he has finished the copywork, invite him to spell any word he remembers. Ask him to spell *love;* if he is unsure, allow him to look at the word.

Track B: Use today and lesson 128 to have your student carefully copy *Hymns in Prose Copybook,* page 58. Allow your student to determine how he wants to divide the work over the two days. Ask him to select a phrase from today's passage to write from memory. Allow him to look at the phrase until he is sure he can spell each word in it correctly.

Lesson 128

Materials Needed
- *More New Friends* (Track A)
- *Hymns in Prose Copybook* (Track B)
- *Hymns in Prose Teacher Book* (Track B, optional)
- Math course of choice

Track A: Have your student read aloud *More New Friends,* pages 152–164, "The Wrong Reward."

Track B: Have your student carefully copy the rest of *Hymns in Prose Copybook,* page 58. Ask him to select a phrase from the passage to write from memory. Allow him to look at the phrase until he is sure he can spell each word in it correctly.

If your student needs more guided reading instruction, spend 15 minutes

simplycharlottemason.com

Notes

working on a lesson from the *Hymns in Prose Teacher Book*.

Math: Work on your selected math curriculum for about 20 minutes.

Lesson 129

Materials Needed
- Math course of choice
- *Spelling Wisdom, Book 1*
- *Using Language Well, Book 1, Student Book*
- *Using Language Well, Book 1, Teacher Guide and Answer Key*
- *Journaling a Year in Nature* notebooks (optional)

Math: Work on your selected math curriculum for about 20 minutes.

English: Complete *Using Language Well, Book 1,* Lesson 52.

Nature Study: Take the whole family outside for nature study.

Lesson 130

Materials Needed
- *Print to Cursive Proverbs* (Track A)
- *Hymns in Prose Copybook* (Track B)
- Math course of choice
- SCM science course of choice

Track A: Have your student read aloud the proverb at the top of *Print to Cursive Proverbs,* page 92, then copy the first part: "Like the glaze covering an earthen vessel".

Track B: Have your student carefully copy *Hymns in Prose Copybook*, page 59. Ask him to select a phrase from the passage to write from memory. Allow him to look at the phrase until he is sure he can spell each word in it correctly.

Math: Work on your selected math curriculum for about 20 minutes.

Science: In your SCM science course, complete the second assignment for Week 26.

Lesson 131

Materials Needed
- *More New Friends,* if needed (Track A)
- Math course of choice
- *Spelling Wisdom, Book 1*
- *Using Language Well, Book 1, Student Book*
- *Using Language Well, Book 1, Teacher Guide and Answer Key*

Track A: Use today to catch up on any assigned reading in *More New Friends,* as needed.

Math: Work on your selected math curriculum for about 20 minutes.

English: Complete *Using Language Well, Book 1,* Lesson 53.

Lesson 132

Materials Needed
- SCM science course of choice
- Math course of choice
- *Print to Cursive Proverbs* (Track A)
- *Hymns in Prose Copybook* (Track B)

Science: In your SCM science course, complete the first assignment for Week 27.

Math: Work on your selected math curriculum for about 20 minutes.

Track A: Have your student read aloud the proverb at the top of *Print to Cursive Proverbs,* page 92, then copy the rest of page 93. When he has finished the copywork, invite him to spell any word he remembers. Ask him to spell *evil*; if he is unsure, allow him to look at the word.

Track B: Use today and lesson 133 to have your student carefully copy *Hymns in Prose Copybook,* page 60. Allow your student to determine how he wants to divide the work over the two days. Ask him to select a phrase from today's passage to write from memory. Allow him to look at the phrase until he is sure he can spell each word in it correctly.

Lesson 133

Materials Needed
- *More New Friends* (Track A)
- *Hymns in Prose Copybook* (Track B)
- *Hymns in Prose Teacher Book* (Track B, optional)
- Math course of choice

Track A: Have your student read aloud *More New Friends,* pages 166–175, "Funny Face."

Track B: Have your student carefully copy the rest of *Hymns in Prose Copybook,* page 60. Ask him to select a phrase from the passage to write from memory. Allow him to look at the phrase until he is sure he can spell each word in it correctly.

If your student needs more guided reading instruction, spend 15 minutes working on a lesson from the *Hymns in Prose Teacher Book.*

TERM

Notes

Math: Work on your selected math curriculum for about 20 minutes.

Lesson 134

Materials Needed
- Math course of choice
- *Spelling Wisdom, Book 1*
- *Using Language Well, Book 1, Student Book*
- *Using Language Well, Book 1, Teacher Guide and Answer Key*
- *Journaling a Year in Nature* notebooks (optional)

Math: Work on your selected math curriculum for about 20 minutes.

English: Complete *Using Language Well, Book 1,* Lesson 54.

Nature Study: Take the whole family outside for nature study.

Lesson 135

Materials Needed
- *Print to Cursive Proverbs* (Track A)
- *Hymns in Prose Copybook* (Track B)
- Math course of choice
- SCM science course of choice

Track A: Have your student complete *Print to Cursive Proverbs,* page 94. When he has finished the copywork, invite him to spell any word he remembers. Ask him to spell *size*; if he is unsure, allow him to look at the word.

Track B: Use today and lesson 137 to have your student carefully copy *Hymns in Prose Copybook,* page 61. Allow your student to determine how he wants to divide the work over the two days. Ask him to select a phrase from today's passage to write from memory. Allow him to look at the phrase until he is sure he can spell each word in it correctly.

Math: Work on your selected math curriculum for about 20 minutes.

Science: In your SCM science course, complete the second assignment for Week 27.

Lesson 136

Materials Needed
- *More New Friends* (Track A)
- Math course of choice
- *Spelling Wisdom, Book 1*
- *Using Language Well, Book 1, Student Book*
- *Using Language Well, Book 1, Teacher Guide and Answer Key*

Track A: Have your student read aloud *More New Friends,* pages 175–183, "A Trip to Town."

Math: Work on your selected math curriculum for about 20 minutes.

English: Complete *Using Language Well, Book 1,* Lesson 55.

Lesson 137

Materials Needed
- SCM science course of choice
- Math course of choice
- *Print to Cursive Proverbs,* if needed (Track A)
- *Hymns in Prose Copybook* (Track B)

Science: In your SCM science course, complete the first assignment for Week 28.

Math: Work on your selected math curriculum for about 20 minutes.

Track A: Use today to catch up on any assigned pages in *Print to Cursive Proverbs,* as needed. If desired, review these words and your student's selected words from previous copywork lessons: *bones, love, evil, size.* If your student is unsure about a particular word's spelling, allow him to look at the word.

Track B: Have your student carefully copy the rest of *Hymns in Prose Copybook,* page 61. Ask him to select a phrase from the passage to write from memory. Allow him to look at the phrase until he is sure he can spell each word in it correctly.

Lesson 138

Materials Needed
- *More New Friends* (Track A)
- *Hymns in Prose Copybook* (Track B)
- *Hymns in Prose Teacher Book* (Track B, optional)
- Math course of choice

Track A: Have your student read aloud *More New Friends,* pages 184–191, "Spoiled Plans."

Track B: Use today and lesson 140 to have your student carefully copy *Hymns in Prose Copybook,* page 62. Allow your student to determine how he wants to divide the work over the two days. Ask him to select a phrase from today's passage to write from memory. Allow him to look at the phrase until he is sure he can spell each word in it correctly.

If your student needs more guided reading instruction, spend 15 minutes working on a lesson from the *Hymns in Prose Teacher Book.*

Notes

Math: Work on your selected math curriculum for about 20 minutes.

Lesson 139

Materials Needed
- Math course of choice
- *Spelling Wisdom, Book 1*
- *Using Language Well, Book 1, Student Book*
- *Using Language Well, Book 1, Teacher Guide and Answer Key*
- *Journaling a Year in Nature* notebooks (optional)

Math: Work on your selected math curriculum for about 20 minutes.

English: Complete *Using Language Well, Book 1*, Lesson 56.

Nature Study: Take the whole family outside for nature study.

Lesson 140

Materials Needed
- *Print to Cursive Proverbs* (Track A)
- *Hymns in Prose Copybook* (Track B)
- Math course of choice
- SCM science course of choice

Track A: Have your student complete *Print to Cursive Proverbs,* page 95.

Track B: Have your student carefully copy the rest of *Hymns in Prose Copybook,* page 62. Ask him to select a phrase from the passage to write from memory. Allow him to look at the phrase until he is sure he can spell each word in it correctly.

Math: Work on your selected math curriculum for about 20 minutes.

Science: In your SCM science course, complete the second assignment for Week 28.

Lesson 141

Materials Needed
- *More New Friends* (Track A)
- Math course of choice
- *Spelling Wisdom, Book 1*
- *Using Language Well, Book 1, Student Book*
- *Using Language Well, Book 1, Teacher Guide and Answer Key*

Track A: Have your student read aloud *More New Friends,* pages 191–199, "A New Game."

Math: Work on your selected math curriculum for about 20 minutes.

English: Complete *Using Language Well, Book 1,* Lesson 57.

Lesson 142

Materials Needed
- SCM science course of choice
- Math course of choice
- *Print to Cursive Proverbs* (Track A)
- *Hymns in Prose Copybook* (Track B)

Science: In your SCM science course, complete the first assignment for Week 29.

Math: Work on your selected math curriculum for about 20 minutes.

Track A: Have your student complete *Print to Cursive Proverbs,* page 96. When he has finished the copywork, invite him to spell any word he remembers. Ask him to spell *even;* if he is unsure, allow him to look at the word.

Tip: It is up to your discretion whether you want to require/review how to form the uppercase letter at the beginning of the words that you will ask your student to spell from memory throughout the rest of the Print to Cursive *lessons. Of course, if you are checking the words' spellings orally, it won't matter.*

Track B: Use today and lesson 143 to have your student carefully copy *Hymns in Prose Copybook,* page 63. Allow your student to determine how he wants to divide the work over the two days. Ask him to select a phrase from today's passage to write from memory. Allow him to look at the phrase until he is sure he can spell each word in it correctly.

Lesson 143

Materials Needed
- *More New Friends,* if needed (Track A)
- *Hymns in Prose Copybook* (Track B)
- *Hymns in Prose Teacher Book* (Track B, optional)
- Math course of choice

Track A: Use today to catch up on any assigned reading in *More New Friends,* as needed.

Track B: Have your student carefully copy the rest of *Hymns in Prose Copybook,* page 63. Ask him to select a phrase from the passage to write from memory. Allow him to look at the phrase until he is sure he can spell each word in it correctly.

simplycharlottemason.com

Notes

If your student needs more guided reading instruction, spend 15 minutes working on a lesson from the *Hymns in Prose Teacher Book.*

Math: Work on your selected math curriculum for about 20 minutes.

Lesson 144

Materials Needed
- Math course of choice
- *Spelling Wisdom, Book 1*
- *Using Language Well, Book 1, Student Book*
- *Using Language Well, Book 1, Teacher Guide and Answer Key*
- *Journaling a Year in Nature* notebooks (optional)

Math: Work on your selected math curriculum for about 20 minutes.

English: Complete *Using Language Well, Book 1,* Lesson 58.

Nature Study: Take the whole family outside for nature study.

Lesson 145

Materials Needed
- *Print to Cursive Proverbs* (Track A)
- *Hymns in Prose Copybook* (Track B)
- Math course of choice
- SCM science course of choice

Track A: Have your student complete *Print to Cursive Proverbs,* page 97. When he has finished the copywork, invite him to spell any word he remembers. Ask him to spell *father;* if he is unsure, allow him to look at the word.

Track B: Use today and lesson 147 to have your student carefully copy *Hymns in Prose Copybook,* page 64. Allow your student to determine how he wants to divide the work over the two days. Ask him to select a phrase from today's passage to write from memory. Allow him to look at the phrase until he is sure he can spell each word in it correctly.

Math: Work on your selected math curriculum for about 20 minutes.

Science: In your SCM science course, complete the second assignment for Week 29.

Lesson 146

Materials Needed
- *More New Friends* (Track A)
- Math course of choice

- *Spelling Wisdom, Book 1*
- *Using Language Well, Book 1, Student Book*
- *Using Language Well, Book 1, Teacher Guide and Answer Key*

Track A: Have your student read aloud *More New Friends,* pages 201–209, "The Wooden Box."

Math: Work on your selected math curriculum for about 20 minutes.

English: Complete *Using Language Well, Book 1,* Lesson 59.

Lesson 147

Materials Needed
- SCM science course of choice
- Math course of choice
- *Print to Cursive Proverbs* (Track A)
- *Hymns in Prose Copybook* (Track B)

Science: In your SCM science course, complete the first assignment for Week 30.

Math: Work on your selected math curriculum for about 20 minutes.

Track A: Have your student complete *Print to Cursive Proverbs,* page 98. When he has finished the copywork, invite him to spell any word he remembers. Ask him to spell *hear;* if he is unsure, allow him to look at the word.

Track B: Have your student carefully copy the rest of *Hymns in Prose Copybook,* page 64. Ask him to select a phrase from the passage to write from memory. Allow him to look at the phrase until he is sure he can spell each word in it correctly.

Lesson 148

Materials Needed
- *More New Friends* (Track A)
- *Hymns in Prose Copybook* (Track B)
- *Hymns in Prose Teacher Book* (Track B, optional)
- Math course of choice

Track A: Have your student read aloud *More New Friends,* pages 209–218, "A Surprise for Toby."

Track B: Use today and lesson 150 to have your student carefully copy *Hymns in Prose Copybook,* page 65. Allow your student to determine how he wants to divide the work over the two days. Ask him to select a phrase from today's passage to write from memory. Allow him to look at the phrase until he is sure he can spell each word in it correctly.

Notes

Notes

If your student needs more guided reading instruction, spend 15 minutes working on a lesson from the *Hymns in Prose Teacher Book*.

Math: Work on your selected math curriculum for about 20 minutes.

Lesson 149

Materials Needed
- Math course of choice
- *Spelling Wisdom, Book 1*
- *Using Language Well, Book 1, Student Book*
- *Using Language Well, Book 1, Teacher Guide and Answer Key*
- *Journaling a Year in Nature* notebooks (optional)

Math: Work on your selected math curriculum for about 20 minutes.

English: Complete *Using Language Well, Book 1,* Lesson 60.

Nature Study: Take the whole family outside for nature study.

Lesson 150

Materials Needed
- *Print to Cursive Proverbs* (Track A)
- *Hymns in Prose Copybook* (Track B)
- Math course of choice
- SCM science course of choice

Track A: Have your student complete *Print to Cursive Proverbs,* page 99. When he has finished the copywork, invite him to spell any word he remembers. Ask him to spell *keep*; if he is unsure, allow him to look at the word.

Track B: Have your student carefully copy the rest of *Hymns in Prose Copybook,* page 65. Ask him to select a phrase from the passage to write from memory. Allow him to look at the phrase until he is sure he can spell each word in it correctly.

Math: Work on your selected math curriculum for about 20 minutes.

Science: In your SCM science course, complete the second assignment for Week 30.

Lesson 151

Materials Needed
- *More New Friends* (Track A)
- Math course of choice
- *Spelling Wisdom, Book 1*

Notes

- Using Language Well, Book 1, Student Book
- Using Language Well, Book 1, Teacher Guide and Answer Key

Track A: Have your student read aloud *More New Friends,* pages 219–226, "Toby and the Teaser."

Math: Work on your selected math curriculum for about 20 minutes.

English: Complete *Using Language Well, Book 1,* Lesson 61.

Lesson 152

Materials Needed
- SCM science course of choice
- Math course of choice
- *Print to Cursive Proverbs* (Track A)
- *Hymns in Prose Copybook* (Track B)

Science: In your SCM science course, complete the first assignment for Week 31.

Math: Work on your selected math curriculum for about 20 minutes.

Track A: Have your student complete *Print to Cursive Proverbs,* page 100. When he has finished the copywork, invite him to spell any word he remembers. Ask him to spell *queen*; if he is unsure, allow him to look at the word.

Track B: Use today and lesson 153 to have your student carefully copy *Hymns in Prose Copybook,* page 66. Allow your student to determine how he wants to divide the work over the two days. Ask him to select a phrase from today's passage to write from memory. Allow him to look at the phrase until he is sure he can spell each word in it correctly.

Lesson 153

Materials Needed
- *More New Friends* (Track A)
- *Hymns in Prose Copybook* (Track B)
- *Hymns in Prose Teacher Book* (Track B, optional)
- Math course of choice

Track A: Have your student read aloud *More New Friends,* pages 226–233, "Billy Bouncer."

Track B: Have your student carefully copy the rest of *Hymns in Prose Copybook,* page 66. Ask him to select a phrase from the passage to write from memory. Allow him to look at the phrase until he is sure he can spell each word in it correctly.

If your student needs more guided reading instruction, spend 15 minutes

Notes

working on a lesson from the *Hymns in Prose Teacher Book*.

Math: Work on your selected math curriculum for about 20 minutes.

Lesson 154

Materials Needed
- Math course of choice
- *Spelling Wisdom, Book 1*
- *Using Language Well, Book 1, Student Book*
- *Using Language Well, Book 1, Teacher Guide and Answer Key*
- *Journaling a Year in Nature* notebooks (optional)

Math: Work on your selected math curriculum for about 20 minutes.

English: Complete *Using Language Well, Book 1*, Lesson 62.

Nature Study: Take the whole family outside for nature study.

Lesson 155

Materials Needed
- *Print to Cursive Proverbs* (Track A)
- *Hymns in Prose Copybook* (Track B)
- Math course of choice
- SCM science course of choice

Track A: Have your student complete *Print to Cursive Proverbs*, page 101. When he has finished the copywork, invite him to spell any word he remembers. Ask him to spell *Rachel*; if he is unsure, allow him to look at the word.

Track B: Use today and lesson 157 to have your student carefully copy the rest of Hymn 10 in *Hymns in Prose Copybook*. Allow your student to determine how he wants to divide the work over the two days. Ask him to select a phrase from today's passage to write from memory. Allow him to look at the phrase until he is sure he can spell each word in it correctly.

Math: Work on your selected math curriculum for about 20 minutes.

Science: In your SCM science course, complete the second assignment for Week 31.

Lesson 156

Materials Needed
- *More New Friends* (Track A)
- Math course of choice
- *Spelling Wisdom, Book 1*

Notes

- *Using Language Well, Book 1, Student Book*
- *Using Language Well, Book 1, Teacher Guide and Answer Key*

Track A: Have your student read aloud *More New Friends*, pages 233–240, "Toby Tries."

Math: Work on your selected math curriculum for about 20 minutes.

English: Complete *Using Language Well, Book 1,* Lesson 63.

Lesson 157

Materials Needed
- SCM science course of choice
- Math course of choice
- *Print to Cursive Proverbs* (Track A)
- *Hymns in Prose Copybook* (Track B)

Science: In your SCM science course, complete the first assignment for Week 32.

Math: Work on your selected math curriculum for about 20 minutes.

Track A: Have your student complete *Print to Cursive Proverbs,* page 102. When he has finished the copywork, invite him to spell any word he remembers. Ask him to spell *better*; if he is unsure, allow him to look at the word.

Track B: Have your student carefully copy the rest of Hymn 10 in *Hymns in Prose Copybook*. If desired, review two or three of your student's selected phrases; see if he can write each phrase correctly as you read it to him.

Lesson 158

Materials Needed
- *More New Friends,* if needed (Track A)
- *Hymns in Prose for Children* (Track B)
- *Hymns in Prose Teacher Book* (Track B, optional)
- Math course of choice

Track A: Use today to catch up on any assigned reading in *More New Friends,* as needed.

Track B: If your student needs more guided reading instruction, spend 15 minutes working on a lesson from the *Hymns in Prose Teacher Book*.
   If he simply needs practice reading, have your student read aloud *Hymns in Prose for Children,* Hymn 11.

Math: Work on your selected math curriculum for about 20 minutes.

simplycharlottemason.com

Notes

Lesson 159

Materials Needed
- Math course of choice
- *Spelling Wisdom, Book 1*
- *Using Language Well, Book 1, Student Book*
- *Using Language Well, Book 1, Teacher Guide and Answer Key*
- *Journaling a Year in Nature* notebooks (optional)

Math: Work on your selected math curriculum for about 20 minutes.

English: Complete *Using Language Well, Book 1,* Lesson 64.

Nature Study: Take the whole family outside for nature study.

Lesson 160

Materials Needed
- *Print to Cursive Proverbs* (Track A)
- *Hymns in Prose Copybook* (Track B)
- Math course of choice
- SCM science course of choice

Track A: Have your student complete *Print to Cursive Proverbs*, page 103. When he has finished the copywork, invite him to spell any word he remembers. Ask him to spell *Joshua*; if he is unsure, allow him to look at the word.

Track B: Have your student carefully copy *Hymns in Prose Copybook,* page 69. Ask him to select a phrase from the passage to write from memory. Allow him to look at the phrase until he is sure he can spell each word in it correctly.

Math: Work on your selected math curriculum for about 20 minutes.

Science: In your SCM science course, complete the second assignment for Week 32.

Lesson 161

Materials Needed
- *More New Friends* (Track A)
- Math course of choice
- *Spelling Wisdom, Book 1*
- *Using Language Well, Book 1, Student Book*
- *Using Language Well, Book 1, Teacher Guide and Answer Key*

Track A: Have your student read aloud *More New Friends,* pages 242–253, "A Friend or an Enemy?"

Math: Work on your selected math curriculum for about 20 minutes.

TERM 3

Notes

English: Complete *Using Language Well, Book 1,* Lesson 65.

Lesson 162

Materials Needed
- SCM science course of choice
- Math course of choice
- *Print to Cursive Proverbs* (Track A)
- *Hymns in Prose Copybook* (Track B)

Science: In your SCM science course, complete the first assignment for Week 33.

Math: Work on your selected math curriculum for about 20 minutes.

Track A: Have your student complete *Print to Cursive Proverbs,* page 104. When he has finished the copywork, invite him to spell any word he remembers. Ask him to spell *if*; if he is unsure, allow him to look at the word.

Track B: Use today and lesson 163 to have your student carefully copy *Hymns in Prose Copybook,* page 70. Allow your student to determine how he wants to divide the work over the two days. Ask him to select a phrase from today's passage to write from memory. Allow him to look at the phrase until he is sure he can spell each word in it correctly.

Lesson 163

Materials Needed
- *More New Friends* (Track A)
- *Hymns in Prose Copybook* (Track B)
- *Hymns in Prose Teacher Book* (Track B, optional)
- Math course of choice

Track A: Have your student read aloud *More New Friends,* pages 254–260, "Two Kinds of Fun."

Track B: Have your student carefully copy the rest of *Hymns in Prose Copybook,* page 70. Ask him to select a phrase from the passage to write from memory. Allow him to look at the phrase until he is sure he can spell each word in it correctly.

If your student needs more guided reading instruction, spend 15 minutes working on a lesson from the *Hymns in Prose Teacher Book.*

Math: Work on your selected math curriculum for about 20 minutes.

simplycharlottemason.com

Notes

Lesson 164

Materials Needed
- Math course of choice
- *Spelling Wisdom, Book 1*
- *Using Language Well, Book 1, Student Book*
- *Using Language Well, Book 1, Teacher Guide and Answer Key*
- *Journaling a Year in Nature* notebooks (optional)

Math: Work on your selected math curriculum for about 20 minutes.

English: Complete *Using Language Well, Book 1,* Lesson 66.

Nature Study: Take the whole family outside for nature study.

Lesson 165

Materials Needed
- *Print to Cursive Proverbs* (Track A)
- *Hymns in Prose Copybook* (Track B)
- Math course of choice
- SCM science course of choice

Track A: Have your student complete *Print to Cursive Proverbs,* page 105. When he has finished the copywork, invite him to spell any word he remembers. Ask him to spell *Samuel*; if he is unsure, allow him to look at the word.

Track B: Have your student carefully copy *Hymns in Prose Copybook,* page 71. Ask him to select a phrase from the passage to write from memory. Allow him to look at the phrase until he is sure he can spell each word in it correctly.

Math: Work on your selected math curriculum for about 20 minutes.

Science: In your SCM science course, complete the second assignment for Week 33.

Lesson 166

Materials Needed
- *More New Friends* (Track A)
- Math course of choice
- *Spelling Wisdom, Book 1*
- *Using Language Well, Book 1, Student Book*
- *Using Language Well, Book 1, Teacher Guide and Answer Key*

Track A: Have your student read aloud *More New Friends,* pages 261–271, "Some Coals That Burn."

Math: Work on your selected math curriculum for about 20 minutes.

English: Complete *Using Language Well, Book 1*, Lesson 67.

Lesson 167

Materials Needed
- SCM science course of choice
- Math course of choice
- *Print to Cursive Proverbs* (Track A)
- *Hymns in Prose Copybook* (Track B)

Science: In your SCM science course, complete the first assignment for Week 34.

Math: Work on your selected math curriculum for about 20 minutes.

Track A: Have your student complete *Print to Cursive Proverbs,* page 106. When he has finished the copywork, invite him to spell any word he remembers. Ask him to spell *Lord God*; if he is unsure, allow him to look at the word.

Track B: Use today and lesson 168 to have your student carefully copy *Hymns in Prose Copybook,* page 72. Allow your student to determine how he wants to divide the work over the two days. Ask him to select a phrase from today's passage to write from memory. Allow him to look at the phrase until he is sure he can spell each word in it correctly.

Lesson 168

Materials Needed
- *More New Friends* (Track A)
- *Hymns in Prose Copybook* (Track B)
- *Hymns in Prose Teacher Book* (Track B, optional)
- Math course of choice

Track A: Have your student read aloud *More New Friends,* pages 271–280, "A Narrow Escape."

Track B: Have your student carefully copy the rest of *Hymns in Prose Copybook,* page 72. Ask him to select a phrase from the passage to write from memory. Allow him to look at the phrase until he is sure he can spell each word in it correctly.

If your student needs more guided reading instruction, spend 15 minutes working on a lesson from the *Hymns in Prose Teacher Book*.

Math: Work on your selected math curriculum for about 20 minutes.

simplycharlottemason.com

Notes

Lesson 169

Materials Needed
- Math course of choice
- *Spelling Wisdom, Book 1*
- *Using Language Well, Book 1, Student Book*
- *Using Language Well, Book 1, Teacher Guide and Answer Key*
- *Journaling a Year in Nature* notebooks (optional)

Math: Work on your selected math curriculum for about 20 minutes.

English: Complete *Using Language Well, Book 1,* Lesson 68.

Nature Study: Take the whole family outside for nature study.

Lesson 170

Materials Needed
- *Print to Cursive Proverbs* (Track A)
- *Hymns in Prose Copybook* (Track B)
- Math course of choice
- SCM science course of choice

Track A: Make 3–5 extra copies of page 107 before your student writes on it. (You will use the copies for some final lessons later.) Then have your student complete *Print to Cursive Proverbs,* page 107, by signing his name.

Track B: Have your student carefully copy *Hymns in Prose Copybook,* page 73. Ask him to select a phrase from the passage to write from memory. Allow him to look at the phrase until he is sure he can spell each word in it correctly.

Math: Work on your selected math curriculum for about 20 minutes.

Science: In your SCM science course, complete the second assignment for Week 34.

Lesson 171

Materials Needed
- *More New Friends* (Track A)
- Math course of choice
- *Spelling Wisdom, Book 1*
- *Using Language Well, Book 1, Student Book*
- *Using Language Well, Book 1, Teacher Guide and Answer Key*

Track A: Have your student read aloud *More New Friends,* pages 280–285, "The Golden Windows."

Math: Work on your selected math curriculum for about 20 minutes.

English: Complete *Using Language Well, Book 1,* Lesson 69.

Lesson 172

Materials Needed
- SCM science course of choice
- Math course of choice
- *Print to Cursive Proverbs,* if needed (Track A)
- *Hymns in Prose Copybook* (Track B)

Science: In your SCM science course, complete the first assignment for Week 35.

Math: Work on your selected math curriculum for about 20 minutes.

Track A: Use today to catch up on any pages of *Print to Cursive Proverbs,* as needed.

Track B: Have your student carefully copy *Hymns in Prose Copybook,* page 74. Ask him to select a phrase from the passage to write from memory. Allow him to look at the phrase until he is sure he can spell each word in it correctly.

Lesson 173

Materials Needed
- *More New Friends,* if needed (Track A)
- *Hymns in Prose Copybook* (Track B)
- *Hymns in Prose Teacher Book* (Track B, optional)
- Math course of choice

Track A: Use the rest of this week and next week to catch up on any assigned reading in *More New Friends,* as needed.

Track B: Have your student carefully copy *Hymns in Prose Copybook,* page 75. Ask him to select a phrase from the passage to write from memory. Allow him to look at the phrase until he is sure he can spell each word in it correctly.

If your student needs more guided reading instruction, spend 15 minutes working on a lesson from the *Hymns in Prose Teacher Book.*

Math: Work on your selected math curriculum for about 20 minutes.

Lesson 174

Materials Needed
- Math course of choice
- *Spelling Wisdom, Book 1*
- *Using Language Well, Book 1, Student Book*
- *Using Language Well, Book 1, Teacher Guide and Answer Key*

simplycharlottemason.com

Notes

- *Journaling a Year in Nature* notebooks (optional)

Math: Work on your selected math curriculum for about 20 minutes.

English: Complete *Using Language Well, Book 1,* Lesson 70.

Nature Study: Take the whole family outside for nature study.

Lesson 175

Materials Needed
- *Print to Cursive Proverbs* and copy of page 107 (Track A)
- *Hymns in Prose Copybook* (Track B)
- Math course of choice
- SCM science course of choice

Track A: Have your student select any proverb from *Print to Cursive Proverbs* and write it in cursive. Use a copy of page 107 for your student to write on.

Track B: Have your student carefully copy *Hymns in Prose Copybook,* page 76. Ask him to select a phrase from the passage to write from memory. Allow him to look at the phrase until he is sure he can spell each word in it correctly.

Math: Work on your selected math curriculum for about 20 minutes.

Science: In your SCM science course, complete the second assignment for Week 35.

Lesson 176

Materials Needed
- *More New Friends,* if needed (Track A)
- Math course of choice
- *Spelling Wisdom, Book 1,* if needed
- *Using Language Well, Book 1, Student Book,* if needed
- *Using Language Well, Book 1, Teacher Guide and Answer Key,* if needed

Track A: Use this week to catch up on any assigned reading in *More New Friends,* as needed.

Math: Work on your selected math curriculum for about 20 minutes.

English: Use today and lesson 179 to catch up on any assigned lessons in *Using Language Well, Book 1,* as needed.

Lesson 177

Materials Needed
- SCM science course of choice

Notes

- Math course of choice
- *Print to Cursive Proverbs* and copy of page 107 (Track A)
- *Hymns in Prose for Children* (Track B)
- *Hymns in Prose Copybook,* if needed (Track B)

Science: In your SCM science course, complete the first assignment for Week 36.

Math: Work on your selected math curriculum for about 20 minutes.

Track A: Have your student select any proverb from *Print to Cursive Proverbs* and write it in cursive. Use a copy of page 107 for your student to write on.

Track B: If he is able, have your student read aloud *Hymns in Prose for Children,* Hymn 12. Also use this week to catch up on any assigned pages in *Hymns in Prose Copybook,* as needed.

Lesson 178

Materials Needed
- *More New Friends,* if needed (Track A)
- *Hymns in Prose for Children* (Track B)
- *Hymns in Prose Copybook,* if needed (Track B)
- *Hymns in Prose Teacher Book* (Track B, optional)
- Math course of choice

Track A: Use today to catch up on any assigned reading in *More New Friends,* as needed.

Track B: If he is able, have your student read aloud *Hymns in Prose for Children,* Hymn 13. Also use this week to catch up on any assigned pages in *Hymns in Prose Copybook,* as needed.
  If your student needs more guided reading instruction, spend 15 minutes working on a lesson from the *Hymns in Prose Teacher Book.*

Math: Work on your selected math curriculum for about 20 minutes.

Lesson 179

Materials Needed
- Math course of choice
- *Spelling Wisdom, Book 1,* if needed
- *Using Language Well, Book 1, Student Book,* if needed
- *Using Language Well, Book 1, Teacher Guide and Answer Key,* if needed
- *Journaling a Year in Nature* notebooks (optional)

Math: Work on your selected math curriculum for about 20 minutes.

TERM

Notes

English: Use today to catch up on any assigned lessons in *Using Language Well, Book 1*, as needed.

Nature Study: Take the whole family outside for nature study.

Lesson 180

Materials Needed
- *Print to Cursive Proverbs* and copy of page 107 (Track A)
- *Hymns in Prose for Children* (Track B)
- *Hymns in Prose Copybook*, if needed (Track B)
- Math course of choice
- SCM science course of choice

Track A: Have your student select any proverb from *Print to Cursive Proverbs* and write it in cursive. Use a copy of page 107 for your student to write on.

Track B: Have your student read aloud *Hymns in Prose for Children*, Hymn 14. Also use today to catch up on any assigned pages in *Hymns in Prose Copybook*, as needed.

Math: Work on your selected math curriculum for about 20 minutes.

Science: In your SCM science course, complete the second assignment for Week 36.